Riding the Leadership Rollercoaster

The Palgrave Kets de Vries Library

Manfred F. R. Kets de Vries, Distinguished Professor of Leadership and Development and Organizational Change at INSEAD, is one of the world's leading thinkers on leadership, coaching, and the application of clinical psychology to individual and organizational change. Palgrave's professional business list operates at the interface between academic rigor and real-world implementation. Professor Kets de Vries's work exemplifies that perfect combination of intellectual depth and practical application and Palgrave is proud to bring almost a decade's worth of work together in the Palgrave Kets de Vries Library.

Sex, Money, Happiness, and Death
The Coaching Kaleidoscope[*]
Mindful Leadership Coaching
Coach and Couch (2nd edition)[†]
You Will Meet a Tall, Dark Stranger
Telling Fairy Tales in the Boardroom
Riding the Leadership Rollercoaster

---

[*] Edited by Manfred F. R. kets de Vries, Laura Guillén, Konstantin Korotov, Elizabeth Florent-Treacy

[†] Edited by Manfred Kets de Vries, Konstantin Korotov, Elizabeth Florent-Treacy, Caroline Rook

Manfred F.R. Kets de Vries

Riding the Leadership Rollercoaster

An observer's guide

Manfred F.R. Kets de Vries
INSEAD
Fontainebleau, France

ISBN 978-3-319-45161-9 ISBN 978-3-319-45162-6 (eBook)
DOI 10.1007/978-3-319-45162-6

Library of Congress Control Number: 2016957771

Cover illustration: Phillip Harris/agencyrush.com

Printed on acid-free paper

This Palgrave Macmillan imprint is published by Springer Nature
The registered company is Springer International Publishing AG
The registered company address is: Gewerbestrasse 11, 6330 Cham, Switzerland

To Joyce McDougall and Maurice Dongier, who helped me to see the potential within myself and guided me on my life's journey.

Foreword

I'm having a great time. It's like I'm on some ridiculous big rollercoaster, not knowing what's happening next, but just having a great time on the ride.

—Samantha Mumba

Challenging the meaning of life is the truest expression of the state of being human.

—Victor Frankl

For most of us, life is a rollercoaster ride, with peaks of joy and valleys of heartache, rather than a long, straight road. Life can be scary and exciting at the same time. It is rife with unpredictable changes and challenges. The rollercoaster effect is particularly apparent to those in leadership positions. They are more likely to experience ups and downs, successes and failures, happy days and sad. The intensity of the experience depends on the "rider." They can scream or enjoy the ride—or, indeed, do both. They can make the best out of the beginnings and endings, the good times and bad, or they can sink beneath them.

Leadership often means living on the edge, living a life less ordinary, leaving the straight and narrow to take a more exciting path. Like riding a rollercoaster, there will be moments that take our breath away but it is in those moments that we feel truly alive. Although we may not know what is coming round the next bend or after the next rise, we have a great time on the ride.

Over the years that I have been a practicing psychoanalyst, management professor, consultant, and executive coach, I have been an observer on the rollercoaster rides taken by thousands of individuals. As I have accompanied them, I have been bombarded with questions, many of which I still struggle to answer. Over time, I have come to accept that being at ease with not having all the answers has its own merit. The short pieces in this book are reflections on the ups and downs of the leadership journey, the distillation of some of my observations over the course of a career. Each piece is followed by questions encouraging readers to reflect on the main themes and how they relate to their own experience, in both their personal and professional lives.

My interest in people's inner theater pervades every aspect of my work. I have always pushed my students and clients to become personal and organizational detectives, to look beyond the obvious and discover the deeper meaning of their own and others' actions. My hope has always been that this kind of knowledge will prevent their becoming prisoners of their own past, failing to recognize the repetitive patterns in their behavior, making the same mistakes over and over again. I want them to develop their self-understanding so that they realize their real potential and recognize their limits. I always have tried to help people to widen their ability to choose. I hope that this book will make a small contribution in this direction.

I would like to thank the people who have helped me write this book. I am grateful to David Champion, senior editor at the *Harvard Business Review*, and Jane Williams, editor at INSEAD Knowledge, for encouraging me to write a series of blogs and short articles, a departure from my usual writing style. I would also like to thank Sally Simmons, my irrepressible editor, who has helped me kill my darlings, knock the book into shape, and steer it to publication. My research associate Alicia Cheak-Baillargeon always surprises me with the speed with which she deals with every task I give her. And last, but certainly not least, I want to express my gratitude to Sheila Loxham, who has been my assistant for more than 20 years, and who tries (not always successfully) to organize my life so that I can devote so much time to my favorite activity. It is probably superfluous to say that any errors or inadequacies in this book are my responsibility alone, and nobody else's.

Contents

About the Author

Manfred F. R. Kets de Vries brings a different view to the much-studied subjects of leadership and the dynamics of individual and organizational change. Bringing to bear his knowledge and experience of economics (Econ. Drs., University of Amsterdam), management (ITP, MBA, and DBA, Harvard Business School), and psychoanalysis (Canadian Psychoanalytic Society, Paris Psychoanalytic Society, and the International Psychoanalytic Association), Kets de Vries scrutinizes the interface between international management, psychoanalysis, psychotherapy, and dynamic psychiatry. His specific areas of interest are leadership, career dynamics, executive stress, entrepreneurship, family business, succession planning, cross-cultural management, team building, coaching, and the dynamics of corporate transformation and change.

The Distinguished Clinical Professor of Leadership Development and Organizational Change at INSEAD, Kets de Vries has been the Founding Director of INSEAD's Global Leadership Center, one of the largest leadership development centers in the world. In addition, he is Program Director of INSEAD's top management program, "The Challenge of Leadership: Creating Reflective Leaders," and Scientific Director of the Executive Master Program "Consulting and Coaching for Change" (and has received INSEAD's distinguished teacher award five times). He has also held professorships at McGill University, the École des Hautes Études Commerciales, Montreal, the European School for Management and Technology, Berlin, and the Harvard Business School, and he has lectured at management institutions around the world.

The *Financial Times*, *Le Capital*, *Wirtschaftswoche*, and *The Economist* have rated Manfred Kets de Vries among the world's leading management thinkers and among the most influential contributors to human resource management.

Kets de Vries is the author, co-author, or editor of more than 40 books, including *The Neurotic Organization, Leaders, Fools and Impostors, Life and Death in the Executive Fast Lane, The Leadership Mystique, The Happiness Equation, Are Leaders Made or Are They Born? The Case of Alexander the Great, The New Russian Business Elite, Leadership by Terror, The Global Executive Leadership Inventory, The Leader on the Couch, Coach and Couch, The Family Business on the Couch, Sex, Money, Happiness, and Death: The Quest for Authenticity*, *Reflections on Leadership and Character, Reflections on Leadership and Career, Reflections on Organizations, The Coaching Kaleidoscope, The Hedgehog Effect: The Secrets of High Performance Teams* and *Mindful Leadership Coaching: Journeys into the Interior*. A new three-book series, The Palgrave Kets de Vries Library, was published in 2015–2016. The titles are: *You Will Meet a Tall Dark Stranger: Executive Coaching Challenges*, *Telling Fairy Tales in the Boardroom: How to Make Sure Your Organization Lives Happily Ever After*, and *Riding the Leadership Rollercoaster: An Observer's Guide*.

In addition, Kets de Vries has published over 400 academic papers as chapters in books and as articles. He has also written approximately 100 case studies, including seven that received the Best Case of the Year award. He is a regular writer for a number of magazines. His work has been featured in such publications as the *New York Times*, the *Wall Street Journal*, the *Los Angeles Times*, *Fortune*, *BusinessWeek*, *The Economist*, the *Financial Times*, the *Harvard Business Review* and the *International Herald Tribune*. His books and articles have been translated into 31 languages. He is a member of 17 editorial boards and has been elected a Fellow of the Academy of Management. He is a founding member of the International Society for the Psychoanalytic Study of Organizations (ISPSO), which has honored him as a lifetime member. Kets de Vries is also the first non-American recipient of ILA Lifetime Achievement Award for his contributions to leadership research and development, being considered one of the world's founding professionals in the development of leadership as a field and discipline. He also received a Lifetime Achievement Award from Germany for his contributions to executive development. The American Psychological Association has honored him with the "Harry and Miriam Levinson Award" (Organizational Consultation division) for his contributions to the field of consultation. Furthermore, he is the recipient of the "Freud Memorial Award" for his contributions at the interface of management and psychoanalysis and the "Vision of Excellence Award" from the Harvard Institute of Coaching. In October 2015 INSEAD made him the first beneficiary of the INSEAD Dominique Héau Award for Inspiring Educational Excellence. He is also the recipient of two honorary doctorates.

Kets de Vries is a consultant on organizational design/transformation and strategic human resource management to leading US, Canadian, European, African, and Asian companies. As a global consultant in executive leadership development his clients have included ABB, ABN-AMRO, Aegon, Air Liquide, Alcan, Alcatel, Accenture, ATIC, Bain Consulting, Bang & Olufsen, Bonnier, BP, Cairn, Deutsche Bank, Ericsson, GE Capital, Goldman Sachs, Heineken, Hudson, HypoVereinsbank, Investec, KPMG, Lego, Liberty Life, Lufthansa, Lundbeck, McKinsey, National Australian Bank, Nokia, Novartis, NovoNordisk, Origin, SABMiller, Shell, SHV, Spencer Stuart, Standard Bank of South Africa, Unilever, and Volvo Car Corporation. As an educator and consultant he has worked in more than 40 countries. In his role as a consultant, he is also the chairman of the Kets de Vries Institute (KDVI: www.kdvi.com), a boutique leadership development consulting firm.

The Dutch government has made Manfred Kets de Vries an Officer in the Order of Oranje Nassau. He was the first fly fisherman in Outer Mongolia and is a member of New York's Explorers Club. In his spare time he can be found in the rainforests or savannas of Central Africa, the Siberian taiga, the Pamir and Altai Mountains, Arnhemland, or within the Arctic Circle.

e-mail: manfred.ketsdevries@insead.edu
websites: www.ketsdevries.com and www.kdvi.com

Part I

Going Down …

1

I Hate My Boss
Toxic Relationships in the Workplace

Alice loved working for the Achristos Corporation until her boss moved to another organization. All the executives at Achristos, including her former boss, had been pleased with her and positive about her future in the company. However, all that changed when her new boss arrived. He viewed Alice very differently. The old chemistry was well and truly gone and he openly disliked the team he inherited. Within 12 months, he had systematically replaced most of Alice's colleagues and implemented a scorched earth policy toward any initiatives he hadn't originated himself. It didn't matter if a project had obvious value to the organization; if it wasn't his brainchild, he wrote it off.

At first, Alice made heroic efforts to get into her boss's good books, even asking him directly what she could do to earn his trust and respect, given that she clearly didn't have them. But her boss had no time for her. He refused to trust her abilities, didn't back her up, and gave her tedious projects to work on. Alice had no opportunity to show herself at her best.

Alice talked to HR and turned to members of the top executive team for help, but while everyone acknowledged the quality of her work and her professionalism, they were not prepared to stick their necks out for her, in case they endangered their own position. With no effective

M.F.R. Kets de Vries, *Riding the Leadership Rollercoaster*,
DOI 10.1007/978-3-319-45162-6_1

support, Alice thought she would go crazy. Her misery at work began to affect her overall well-being. She became depressed, prone to anxiety attacks, had problems sleeping, and developed bad eating habits. She still loved Achristos but she hated her boss. For the sake of her health, she was going to have to quit.

Unfortunately, Alice's is not a rare story. As the saying goes, people join companies but leave their bosses. Survey data about workforce engagement are disturbing: only 13% of employees worldwide are engaged at work; most—63%—are "not engaged" and 24% are "actively disengaged." In the USA, 50% of employees have quit their jobs to get away from their boss at some point in their career,[1] which makes it the number one reason for leaving an organization. This sounds frankly scandalous, so why don't we hear more about it? We can blame our talent for concealment and rationalization. We might be more ready to give excuses for quitting that don't reflect negatively on ourselves: the children don't like their school, our partner wants to live in another city, we need to be closer to our elderly parents, and so on. But if we press people a little further, the real reason is often incompatibility with the boss.

A lot of people don't trust or respect their bosses and the same grievances are often cited: micro-management, bullying, conflict avoidance, decision paralysis, inconsistent behavior, bosses who take all the credit, bosses who blame others for mistakes, unwillingness to share information, failing to listen, failing to set an example, low-level functioning, and not developing their people. This is quite some list of dysfunctional behavior and it's not exhaustive. Too many people work for the boss from hell and too many organizations pay the price for it. Bad bosses are bad for people and bad for business.

Of course, most bosses are not inherently bad and, as so often in human life, there are always two sides to a story. There may be rational reasons why bosses behave the way they do. They are often under immense pressure to adopt a short-term orientation at the expense of long-term considerations, which can only lead to dysfunctional organizational outcomes.

---

[1] 2013, 142-country Gallup "State of the Global Workplace."

But whatever the reasons, rational or otherwise, what can you do if you find yourself working for a boss you hate? Will you feel you have to walk, like Alice, or can you find another solution?

The fact is that managing your boss is part of your job and doing it well is a key indicator of how effective you are as an executive. If your relationship with your boss is toxic, the first thing to do is to find out whether it's personal, or whether others are having the same experience. If your colleagues also hate your boss, you are faced with a serious situation. One approach could be to get together to devise a group strategy to get rid of your boss. But if others don't have the same experience, you may be part of the problem yourself. This is not something you will want to hear, but if you can acknowledge it, you may be able to make changes in your own behavior that could salvage the relationship.

If you think you are a part of the problem, ask your colleagues what they do differently from you that helps them get on with your boss. This could give you some pointers on how to adjust your approach. If you are politically astute and tactful about this—in terms of who you ask and how you describe the situation—some of these colleagues could act as behind-the-scenes channels to help broker a change in your relationship with your boss.

Another strategy is to observe the people who work successfully with your boss. What do they do that you don't? Have they worked out which of your boss's buttons not to press? More discreet questioning could help you work this out but take care how you go about it: avoid badmouthing your boss, which could rebound on you badly, and frame all questions positively.

Also, try stepping back and taking an objective look at your own feelings and responses. Why do you hate your boss? Is it the way your boss looks, sounds, behaves, or speaks to you? Does your boss remind of anyone else you have felt similar dislike for, either now or in the past? It's worth doing some serious soul-searching about it. You may discover that you have had repeated problems with specific authority figures. Your boss may be a stand-in figure for other problematic people in your life. Psychoanalysts call this a transference reaction, as no relationship is a new relationship; every relationship is colored by previous relationships. You may be subject to a confusion in time, space, and person.

A deeper understanding of interpersonal dynamics may guide you toward having a serious conversation with your boss about why things are not working between the two of you. Poor communication can be a major factor in toxic relationships and starting a conversation might clear the air. You might discover that your boss is not even aware of how unhappy you are. Talking can clarify misunderstandings and may lead to changes in behavior on both sides.

If, having tried all these strategies, it is clear that the root of the problem is not a misunderstanding but a serious personality clash, your options for action are limited. Forget about going to HR, which is (in many instances) there to serve the needs of top management rather than individual employees. The hard fact is that whistle-blowers are generally seen as troublemakers, and eased out of the organization.

You could take a passive response and join the army of the disengaged—just go through the motions at work and minimize contact with your boss. There is always the possibility, or hope, that your boss will move on. But is it really worth hanging in there, growing increasingly disengaged and disenchanted with the job? Like Alice, you run the risk of your misery at work spilling over into all areas of your life, leading to depression and a whole range of other psychosomatic reactions.

One proactive response is to go for broke, approach your boss's boss and ask for a short off-the-record chat. It may be the last thing you do in the company, but at least you will have signaled to senior management that something is very wrong.

If you have failed in every possible attempt to make your relationship with your boss work, start to look for another job. Taking this decision will help safeguard your mental health. In most instances, it's better to prepare an exit strategy while you are still employed. So, beef up your résumé, contact some headhunters, and get some good references lined up. And remember that bad bosses can define you, they can destroy you, but they can also strengthen you. Having a bad boss isn't necessarily your fault, but it will be your fault if you stay with one.

Questions

- Does your boss remind you of any people in your life?
- What feelings and fantasies do you have when dealing with your boss? What effect does your boss have on you?
- Do you believe that you and your boss are acting out some predetermined scenario? Do you understand what roles both of you are playing?
- Do you have an idea about what drives your boss (what makes your boss feel mad, sad, bad, or glad)?
- Have you ever made a serious effort to put yourself in your boss's shoes?
- Have you talked to other people about how they perceive your boss?

2

Riding for a Fall

Hubris—It's Really Real

Antonio del Porte—"Tonio"—was a rising star in the organization. The first thing everyone commented on when they met him was his self-assertion. In any meeting, formal or informal, he spoke out with total confidence. His repeated claim that he knew how to get results, and would get them, was very convincing. He certainly attracted a lot of attention upwards in the organization. If one or two thought he "talked big" and found him smug and overbearing, for the others he could do no wrong. It was generally accepted that he was headed for a very senior position.

At closer quarters, working with Tonio was a different story. He bounced between teams and was not an easy fit in any of them. He also managed to upset nearly everyone he worked with, some more seriously than others. People complained that he grabbed all the credit, never acknowledged other people's contributions, blamed others when mistakes were made, and managed never to be wrong himself. They agreed he was "a bighead" and "a bit full of himself." Others had worse to report. Tonio was "a bully" who made people afraid to disagree with him and deliberately put them down. He made personal comments about their education, the car they drove, their appearance, their hair loss. He would

M.F.R. Kets de Vries, *Riding the Leadership Rollercoaster*,
DOI 10.1007/978-3-319-45162-6_2

home in on their weak spots and could be downright cruel. Nobody who was present ever forgot the snide comment he made about "special needs" to a team member whose child had Down's syndrome. Yet this and other incidents seemed to go unremarked by his bosses.

To the frustration of Tonio's colleagues and direct reports, many people further up the organization had limitless admiration for him. They couldn't see what he was really like. No notice seemed to be taken of the departure rate among his colleagues and the fact that the areas he worked in were becoming increasingly unproductive. Tonio had a talent for getting moved out and away before the shit really hit the fan and managed to convince everyone that it had nothing to do with him.

Tonio's rise was inexorable and in due course he was promoted to head up a regional operation. Once away from the surveillance that had kept him partly in check, his behavior became intolerable. He dropped the pally "Tonio" and all pretense with it. Visitors to the regional office were struck by the subdued and subservient attitude of the staff. One reported back to head office that she noticed people went out of their way to avoid del Porte and that no one would make eye contact with him in the meeting she attended. Over drinks, someone had told her that del Porte had threatened one of his colleagues with a baseball bat. She hadn't believed a word of it—but began to have doubts when she herself saw the bat in del Porte's office a couple of days later.

The rumors about del Porte began to accumulate but most remained hearsay, as people were too afraid to speak out. His threatening behavior, punitive gestures toward those unlucky enough to cross him, and the plummeting performance figures—somehow he managed to deflect every charge. He seemed invulnerable.

In the end, del Porte overstretched himself. A junior employee reported his aggressive sexual advances to her father, who happened to be a local police inspector. His impromptu appearance, with back up, in del Porte's office the following morning effectively put an end to his reign of terror.

Many narcissistic people, propelled by their drive for power, prestige, fame, and glamor, end up in leadership positions in politics or business. Many of them have been phenomenally successful. Their confidence and ability to influence others serve them well. Unfortunately, over time the darker side of narcissism can make these leaders extremely dysfunctional.

As humans we tend to idealize our leaders. This is a hangover of our need to recreate the sense of security we felt as children, when we still thought our parents were perfect and all-powerful. As a result, as adults we may endow our leaders with unrealistic strengths and abilities and project our feelings of fear and admiration onto them. It's a rare person who can resist this kind of admiration. Many leaders begin to believe that they really are everything their people want them to be. They gradually fall victim to what the Greeks called *hubris*—excessive pride and self-confidence—and develop a sense of entitlement. Contemptuous and impatient toward everyone less wonderful than themselves, they react with disdain, rage, or vindictiveness toward anything they don't like and anyone who seems likely to enjoy similar success.

Antonio del Porte's story did not have the sort of dramatic dénouement that an office full of police might suggest. He was too good at getting away with things. Instead, he took the initiative, contacting head office while the police were still in his room to announce his immediate resignation and leaving the building as soon as he had done so. Over the next 24 hours he had sorted out a suitable severance package and cut a deal to preclude any charges being brought. Four months later, the business press noted that del Porte had been catapulted into the post of regional head for a different organization in a different market. It seemed he also had a talent for creating smokescreens.

After only 19 months in post, the damage del Porte left behind him was considerable. Once he had gone, a stream of accusations of abuse and misconduct followed. Morale in the regional office was at an all-time low—del Porte's conduct had been tolerated for so long, and the reasons for his departure remained very opaque: how could the judgment of other leaders in the organization be trusted? And as the bullying behavior had cascaded down through the organization, it had had a serious impact on the bottom line. Suppliers had fallen away and staff had either become largely non-functioning or engaged in acts of sabotage—self-protective or vengeful responses to the prevailing culture. Job losses were inevitable;

equally serious was the loss of the organization's credibility in local markets. It took far longer than 19 months for it to regain the position it had enjoyed before del Porte took over.

So what can you do if you are stuck with a Tonio in the workplace? Happily, nowadays atrocities are increasingly difficult to hide on both the world stage and smaller forums, what with the ubiquity of 24-hour news and social media. In the worst cases, faced with an Assad or Gaddafi, for example, outside intervention seems to be the only way to deal with an offender. In the workplace, however, this can be less straightforward. Narcissists are notoriously resistant to the sort of coaching or consulting interventions aimed at altering their dysfunctional behavior.

Ideally, an organization should be aware of the darker side of narcissism and have set up systems to nip any signs of it in the bud. Unfortunately, many organizational cultures provide fertile soil for hubris; it is too easy to turn a blind eye to the wrong kind of behavior if it gets the right results. But when the best people start to leave and the organization is left with collaborators, flatterers, and others without the skills or experience to be able to look elsewhere, it is in deep trouble. Getting out while the going is good is a straightforward option for individuals. Other options might require more imagination.

I once heard about a female executive whose erratic and unreasonable behavior infuriated and terrorized her colleagues; however, she was exceptionally good at her job and her reputation in the sector brought real kudos to the company. Her aggression was legendary but so also was a less alarming weakness—she felt the cold and because of this kept a bulky knitted cardigan in her office that she took off only for important meetings. After a while a rumor began to circulate that there was a secret URL devoted to this "comfy cardi" to which those savaged by its owner had exclusive access. Joiners discovered that the URL consisted simply of people photographed posing in the cardigan and included the CEO, the head of security, and the post room staff, as well as most of the executive's direct reports. Knowledge of this URL became a kind of invisible armor for the executive's victims—laughter and solidarity can be excellent forms of defense.

Questions

- Does your organization turn a blind eye to people who produce great results but don't live the organization's values?
- Are some people in your organization (including yourself) attracted to being in the limelight? Are there other behavior patterns that characterize these people?
- Are there people in your organization who show excessive self-confidence combined with contempt for advice or criticism of others?
- Does your organization have checks and balances for people who feel and behave as if they are special?
- Do you have people in your organization that have a healthy disrespect for their boss—individuals who are prepared to tell their seniors and/or colleagues uncomfortable things? Is this kind of behavior an essential part of your organizational culture?

3

Why Them and Not Me?

Dealing with the Problem of Envy

As VP of Quality Control of a global pharmaceutical company, Fabienne was notorious for the way she radiated negativity. Angry and highly irritable, she ran other people down, begrudged them their positions in the company, disparaged their intelligence, and never acknowledged their achievements. She made no attempt to hide her resentment of others' success. If someone challenged her attitude, she would retaliate, rationalizing or intellectualizing her behavior.

Unsurprisingly, complaints were made about Fabienne from both inside and outside the organization. She was building up a damaging reputation for herself, not helped by her excessive drinking and drug abuse, a form of self-medication that helped control the envy that was poisoning her life. Eventually the company had had enough and Fabienne was fired—for the second time in five years.

Maybe you have come across a Fabienne. Have you ever met someone whose obvious envy made you feel uncomfortable? Have you felt threatened by the comments or behavior of an envious person? Maybe Fabienne is uncomfortably familiar: do you have problems with envy yourself? Are you preoccupied by other people's accomplishments?

M.F.R. Kets de Vries, *Riding the Leadership Rollercoaster*,
DOI 10.1007/978-3-319-45162-6_3

The psychoanalyst Carl Jung would refer to the "shadow," the hidden, repressed parts of ourselves that we refuse to acknowledge. It is as if envy blinds insight, undermines a person's sense of self, and complicates human interaction. It can have devastating consequences in social settings.

Envy means literally to look against or to look with ill will toward another person. It refers to discontent felt at the good fortune of someone else—feeling good when other people fail. It is one of our most powerful dark emotions, a painful blend of inferiority, hostility, and resentment that arises when we see someone else with something we deeply want and makes us want to spoil the things we covet.

There are very good reasons why envy is one of the traditional "seven deadly sins." It has the power to blind our judgment and spoil our relationships. It's also one of the sins that bring no pleasure to the sinner, except for the twisted pleasure of *Schadenfreude*, that feeling of delight when bad things happen to those we envy. Shame and guilt are envy's natural companions. They deepen the misery of envy but also encourage us to find ways to hide it, which makes it a difficult problem to identify and deal with.

It is actually impossible to avoid envy. There will always be someone who has something we desire and from that point of view it is an inevitable part of the human experience. Under some conditions, envy can even be a good thing. When we admire someone to the extent of wanting to be like them, envy becomes "constructive." In signaling an unfulfilled need, envy can be a great motivating force.

Mostly, however, envy is destructive. A persistent feeling that other people have something we want results in incessant social comparisons that threaten our self-image. We feel deficient, dissatisfied, and inadequate and in response become resentful toward others we perceive as successful, because they have money, power, status, beauty, luck, or are simply happy. Envy hurts and causes profound misery. Envy damages relationships, disrupts teams, and undermines organizational performance. It also damages the envious person. It has been linked to several forms of maladjustment, such as poor interpersonal relations, low self-esteem, depression, anxiety, anger issues, and even criminal behavior.

In spite of this, all is not lost. Envy can be mastered if we change our perceptions, refocusing on how to be happy with what we have.

Returning to Fabienne, her attitude had seen her kicked out of two jobs in relatively quick succession and she couldn't ignore such a loud wake-up call. She had to acknowledge the extent to which her envious feelings were affecting her emotional and physical health. Encouraged by one of the few friends she had left, she decided to get help from an executive coach.

Having made the decision, Fabienne found it easier than she had expected to talk about her envy. She couldn't help comparing herself to others and always feeling short-changed. All her life she had had the sense that she'd got the sticky end of the lollipop and everyone else had come in for the abilities, virtues, values, and attributes she wanted. She would obsess about people she perceived as rivals and grew angry and vindictive toward them. She knew she was a "spoiler" and admitted that spoiling made feel her feel better, until shame and guilt took over. Her envy for her own husband's career had also affected their marriage, because it gave her more pleasure when he failed than when he did well. She resented having to celebrate her friends' achievements: any promotion, wedding, birth of a child, or house move hurt her bitterly. She didn't really want to make those deflating comments, but she couldn't help herself.

Fabienne was not stupid. She knew her toxic behavior was poisoning herself. She didn't want to be the kind of person she was, but could see no way of working toward self-improvement. She was locked into trying to eliminate whatever she perceived as "competition" and had no energy left for anything else.

At first, the coach encouraged Fabienne to get her envious feelings under control by monitoring her thoughts carefully and taking time to figure out whether they were envious. It was important for Fabienne to catch and correct her thinking processes and to minimize her envy before it became full-blown.

This exercise helped Fabienne to identify a developmental cause for her unhappiness. She was well aware of her envy toward her sister, whom she believed had been their mother's favorite daughter. She realized that this pivotal relationship was at the core of her problems. As a result, there were too many preferred "sisters" in her life. In many ways, hers was a classic case. Envious feelings are a legacy of early comparisons made within the family context. The basic scenario is that envious people end up with the lingering feeling that they got a rough deal compared to other members of the family. Any physical, intellectual, or emotional deficiencies obviously accentuate these feelings of inferiority.

The coach helped Fabienne to use this insight to refocus on the positive rather than the negative dynamics in her family. She and her sister had shared many good experiences. Capturing these memories was a step forward in establishing a more balanced and healthy perspective.

As the coaching sessions continued, Fabienne learned to control her tendency to assume she was being wronged in every situation in which she found herself. She stopped obsessing over the unfair advantages others enjoyed and learned to appreciate and cultivate her own qualities. She no longer emphasized the bad qualities of others to allow herself to legitimize her feelings of envy. She became less obsessed with other people's success. She tried to improve herself rather than downgrade others. She also became more generous toward herself. The self-confidence this gave her enabled her to pick herself up, get her career firmly back on track, and start to rebuild her relationships with family and friends.

Questions

- Has envy been a pattern throughout your life? Do you have an idea where your feelings of envy come from?
- Under what situations do you feel (most) envious?
- What have you done (if anything) to deal with your envious feelings?
- Are people in your organization held back because of other people's envy?
- Are you able (when you feel envious) to reflect on your own strengths and accomplishments?
- Does your organization have a culture where people are willing to share their accomplishments instead of seeing it as a zero-sum game?
- Are you prepared to make efforts to improve yourself instead of talking down others?

4

Gimme, Gimme, Gimme
The Greed Syndrome

Pavel felt that he had had a good day. At the most recent board meeting of the Raler Company, he had managed to push through a salary and bonus packet worth $20 million. He was quite pleased with the fact that his CEO-to-worker pay ratio stood now at 400:1. But in spite of his formidable pay packet, it niggled him that some of his colleagues in other listed companies were making more than he was. All was not lost, however. He had other irons in the fire. His purchase of the most advanced Gulfstream corporate jet made him feel better—at least for the moment. Raler had also paid for his New York penthouse apartment, and aside from these financial windfalls, he had a generous expense account. The way he had set it up gave him unrestricted opportunities to claim for many personal items, including yacht rental of $20,000 the previous summer.

Despite these luxuries and perks, Pavel continued to question whether he didn't deserve more, given the amount of time he put into his work. Considering what he contributed to the company, he felt that, financially, he was being treated unfairly. It was a familiar feeling. And he still wasn't a member of the billion-dollar club. How was he going to reach that milestone?

M.F.R. Kets de Vries, *Riding the Leadership Rollercoaster*,
DOI 10.1007/978-3-319-45162-6_4

Life, as we know, is full of surprises. In the middle of a heated discussion about a takeover bid, from which he stood to make a real financial bundle, Pavel had a stroke. For a short time, he was kept alive on life support, but his eventual death put an end to his sense of never having enough. For Pavel, life without money had always seemed absurd, but money without life turned out to be quite pointless. The greed syndrome comes with a price.

Pavel is a good example of the greed and excess that are the hallmarks of many executives. Greed is a characteristic that cuts across most human endeavors and has done for as long as our species has existed. But throughout human history, greed has had a very mixed press. Philosophers have struggled with the question of how much greed a society can tolerate. Although greed has been hailed as the motor of economic growth and human progress, uncontrolled greed has been seen as the cause of much misery, as recent economic history has shown dramatically. In spite of these examples, our culture continues to place a high value on materialism, and, by extension, greed. But luckily, there are some clear warning signs of uncontrolled greed.

Overly self-centered behavior is the first giveaway of greedy people. This kind of behavior is typified by Ebenezer Scrooge, the anti-hero of Charles Dickens's novel *A Christmas Carol.* Scrooge is a stingy, greedy businessman who has no place in his life for kindness, compassion, charity, or benevolence. Greedy people are always saying "me, me, me," with very little regard for the needs and feelings of others.

Envy is another clue. Envy and greed are like twins. While greed can be defined as an excessive desire for possessions (such as wealth and power), envy can be defined as an extreme desire to get what belongs to others. Envy goes one step further than greed, in that it induces a strong desire among greedy people for the possessions of others.

Greedy people struggle with the concept of empathy. Caring—being concerned about the feelings of others—is not part of their repertoire. They find it very difficult to relate to what other people feel and have few qualms about causing pain to others. Their inability to empathize, their lack of genuine interest in the ideas and feelings of others, and their unwillingness to take personal responsibility for their behavior and actions when things do not work out, makes them very difficult people to be with.

The world is a zero-sum game for the greedy. Instead of thinking that everyone will benefit if the pie gets larger, they view the pie as a constant. They are not into sharing; they always want to have the biggest part of the pie. They are never satisfied. They believe that they deserve more, even if it comes at someone else's expense. They are also the kind of people who will bite the hand that feeds them.

Greedy people are also very quick to take credit for work done by others. They excel at maximizing their contributions and minimizing the work of others. They are masters of manipulation. They can be charming but their principal agenda is to have people around who will feed their ego. However, as "takers" (rather than "givers"), whatever they do, they don't feel good for very long.

Short-termism is another warning sign. Greedy people are focused on sating their immediate needs. Their greediness compels them to do anything to get what they believe is rightfully theirs, whatever the consequences, which anyway will be someone else's responsibility to deal with. As leaders of corporations, they are more interested in getting their bonuses instead of making investments for future innovation, or sharing whatever benefits accrue with their employees.

Finally, greedy people are not good at maintaining boundaries. In the pursuit of their material needs, they know no limits. They will compromise moral values and ethics to achieve their goals—cheating included. For personal gain, they look for loopholes or clever ways to outsmart the rules and regulations that have been put in place to moderate this kind of behavior.

I have learned from long experience of dealing with greedy executives that foolish decisions motivated by greed can become blessings in disguise. Often, serious personal setbacks expose the self-destructive course they are following and create the opening that greedy people need to be able to change. Health issues or serious relationship problems may also propel them to confront their addiction to greed.

To create the motivation to change, greedy people may have to go on an inner journey (perhaps accompanied by a coach or therapist) to uncover the unconscious sources of their obsessive pursuit of wealth. This may imply dealing with childhood events they experienced that make them behave the way they do. They may have to deal with unresolved conflict, cope with pent-up emotions and anger, work through unfulfilled dreams, and confront the various defenses that drive them toward excess. It also implies being able to distinguish what is really essential in life, including love, emotional intimacy, unconditional acceptance (and self-acceptance), and satisfyingly "rich" relationships. When they embark on such a complex inner journey, some may realize that their obsession with wealth will never bring them the fulfillment they so desperately want.

It's important that greedy people recognize that they have a choice. This means stepping back and asking themselves whether they have other options than mindlessly following their cravings for more. People suffering from the greed syndrome need to find ways to move from egotistic to altruistic striving. They need to experience for themselves that kindness trumps greed; that we can only be rich if we are able to give. Taking this altruistic route requires persistence, patience, humility, courage, and commitment. The penalty for not doing so, however, can cost far more, as Pavel discovered the hard way.

The bigger question we should ask ourselves is how can we change a society that puts so much value on acquisition and excess? The philosopher Arthur Schopenhauer once said, "Wealth is like seawater; the more we drink, the thirstier we become." If we learn how to overcome greed, we may find the key to a simpler, more meaningful, happier, and ultimately richer life.

Questions

- Do you find it difficult to consider other people's needs? Are you always preoccupied with your own?
- Do you reciprocate when others do things for you? Do others accuse you of being self-centered?
- Do you constantly feel that what you have is not enough—that you deserve more—that you deserve special treatment? Do you look for loopholes to get the best out of every situation?
- Do you look at everything you do as a zero-sum game?

- Do you have a tendency to tear others down rather than build them up? Do you do this because it makes you feel better?
- Are you a "Band-Aid" person, always looking for short-term, convenient solutions? Or are you prepared to choose the hard way, taking the bigger picture into consideration?

5

Feeling Sorry for the Super-Rich? A Nasty Case of Affluenza

In my professional encounters, I have met many extremely wealthy individuals who suffer from affluenza, or wealth fatigue syndrome. The main symptoms of this condition are a relentless quest for material gain—money, possessions, appearances (physical and social), and fame—and paradoxically, also misery. Their acquisitions and conspicuous consumption fail to make affluenza sufferers happy. In fact, they can experience a range of psychological disorders, including feelings of alienation and deep distress. The typical symptoms of affluenza are workaholism, depression, lack of motivation, an inability to delay gratification or tolerate frustration, and a false sense of entitlement.

Peter was an extremely successful entrepreneur but his start in life was not auspicious. His father left the family when Peter was only five years old and provided no further financial support to his mother. Fortunately, his maternal grandfather—a jack of all trades—took an interest in the little boy and encouraged his entrepreneurial drive. By the time he was in his early thirties, Peter had become what is usually described as obscenely rich. He had more money than he could have spent over several lifetimes.

And spend it he did. He bought houses, cars, a yacht, and an airplane. But all these acquisitions were like toys: after he'd played with them for

M.F.R. Kets de Vries, *Riding the Leadership Rollercoaster*,
DOI 10.1007/978-3-319-45162-6_5

a while, he lost interest and looked around for something else to spend his money on. Nothing was ever enough—neither money nor what he could buy with it. It was like an addiction. Each acquisition fed his need to acquire—and necessitated more money to do so. Such frenetic pursuit of money can be an attempt to cover up boredom or depression and this was certainly the case with Peter.

Women were just another commodity for Peter. Many were drawn to his wealth and after a number of extra-marital affairs, he left his wife for a much younger woman. This first "quickie" divorce turned out to be rather expensive. After Peter's third marriage (and divorce), he decided that marriage wasn't for him. Three marriages had left quite a mess behind them, including bitter ex-wives and a trail of unhappy children. This made him even more miserable.

Money matters and it would be disingenuous to claim otherwise. We all need a minimal amount of money simply to get by in day-to-day life. But money can become a burden if, like Peter, however much you have never seems to be enough. Although people suffering from affluenza may define themselves in terms of their earnings, possessions, appearance, and celebrity, ironically, having these things can make them more miserable than ever. Are the relationships they have with the people who surround them genuine or parasitic? Are they attractive because of who they are or what they have?

I have dealt with many money-driven executives and I have seen the darker side of immense wealth. One person once asked me, in all seriousness, "What good is money if it can't inspire envy and terror in your fellow man?" Making lots of money can be a deliberate attempt to generate envy in others, and as might be expected, this kind of behavior is like a matador's cape, bringing out the worst in those provoked. But it seems many people would rather be envied than pitied. If money can't buy you friends, it can at least get you a better class of enemy.

If the annual Forbes list of the richest people in the world is anything to go by, large figures are a great way to impress other people. Getting on that list—the destination of many a narcissistic journey—is a highly effective, if not very sophisticated, way of gaining the admiration (or envy) of others. For many of the super-rich, finding they are not featured on the Forbes list is both a personal catastrophe and the ultimate challenge. But even those who make it onto the list can find reasons to torture themselves: is their ranking high enough? After all, for all but one person in the world, there is always someone higher up. Even getting the number-one spot brings limited satisfaction; no one stays there forever, which is why those lists are renewed every year.

We all know that growing up in poverty can affect a child's physical and psychological development; but from the stories I have been told, it seems that growing up surrounded by huge wealth can also be detrimental to the healthy development of the children of the super-rich. A typical scenario is that super-rich parents, busy with the acquisition and management of their wealth, compensate for their unavailability by giving their children presents and money; in essence, money substitutes for love. But children need their parents' presence more than presents. Children raised on this model generally develop ambivalent feelings toward their caretakers: without that solid emotional base, they are unsure whether their caretakers really care about them. Are they only doing whatever they are doing because of their wealth? The result is depression and feelings of insecurity that start in childhood and last into adulthood.

Another complication is that people find it difficult to deal with rich kids, whose upbringing may give them very little sense of how the rest of the world lives. These two factors—their own ignorance of the real world and the discomfort other people feel interacting with them—exacerbate the struggle to establish significant relationships. While most of us would cheerfully sing along with the Beatles' "Money can't buy me love," some rich kids try to make the purchase anyway.

But what about Peter, a serial quitter of families, bobbing about in the wake of three failed marriages with garages full of luxury cars and an eye-wateringly expensive property portfolio? How could he break the cycle of acquisition and dissatisfaction that had cost him so much more than money? How could he change his behavior? Although Peter may have seen the pursuit of money as the road to freedom—given his childhood experiences—following that road had made him a slave to acquisition. It had led him to forfeit the essential things in life. Instead of building relationships and attending to his emotional and psychological health, he would stay late at the office doing things he disliked, to be able to buy things he didn't need, to impress people he didn't really care about.

Peter needed to see that the only cure for affluenza is to start giving back. Ultimately, what makes us lastingly happy is not what we have but what we do. If he could adjust his focus and think what he could do for others, rather than for himself, the quality of his life would start to improve. As a very rich man, this change in focus could be accompanied by substantial altruism; he had the means to be able to make a real difference. Many studies have shown that altruistic acts are good for our emotional well-being and can measurably enhance our peace of mind. Altruistic acts, whether grand or humble, make us feel more contented and fulfilled. There is a great correlation between doing good and feeling good. Giving is good for our mental and physical health. When we give to others, they feel closer to us, and we feel closer to them.

In a film that is consistently voted one of the greatest of all time, *Citizen Kane*, we follow the story of the super-rich Charles Foster Kane, a character based on the American newspaper magnate William Randolph Hearst. The film follows Kane's rise and subsequent fall, when he dies alone in a mansion displaying his monstrous wealth, muttering the enigmatic word "Rosebud." The film's central device is one reporter's fruitless search for the meaning of this word. In the end, we find out that, despite all his wealth, Kane's most enduring memory was of the sled he had been playing with as a child on the day his mother sent him away to school, against his wishes. "Rosebud" is the name stenciled on the sled, which we see discarded on the top of a bonfire as the film ends.

With luck, Peter won't end up like Kane, only recognizing the price he has paid for his unhappiness when it is too late to do anything about it. With the right support, he may learn to value intangibles, like friendship and family ties, take pleasure in the small things of life, and feel the true satisfaction that comes from giving.

Questions

- Are appearances (fame, money, possessions) very important to you?
- Has the act of acquiring things turned into an anti-depressant for you? Do these acquisitions make you feel (temporarily) better?

- Do your acquisitions never feel good enough? Do you always want more?
- Have you ever thought about changing your lifestyle? Have you tried to find other ways to feel better about yourself?
- Are you willing to accept that more is not necessarily better?
- Have you ever made efforts to give back to others instead of spending your time on increased spending—giving only to yourself?

6

It's Not My Fault

The Problem of Denialism

Having geared himself up to tell Tom, his boss, that he had made a terrible mistake in firing the head of IT, Steve realized that he was wasting his time. There was no way his boss was going to accept that it was his own decision that had had such a costly and devastating effect on the organization. Its result was genuine chaos, a walkout of some of the most capable people in the department, and a temporary lockdown of the company's key operations. Yet Tom persisted in denying that he had made a mistake. Everybody knew there had been problems in the IT department but equally everybody knew that the head of IT wasn't the person responsible. The problem lay with one of the company's sub-contractors—a consulting firm that Tom had brought in. But Tom still refused to listen to what Steve had to say and despite the alarming aftermath insisted that he had made the right decision. The head of IT had never been up to the job and he should have fired him much earlier. According to him, Steve was exaggerating when he pointed out that the company had almost gone into the red. In fact, Steve should hold himself responsible for the mess as he'd introduced the head of IT in the first place.

For Steve, this latest debacle confirmed that there was a pattern to Tom's behavior. Far too often Tom had clearly made wrong decisions

M.F.R. Kets de Vries, *Riding the Leadership Rollercoaster*,
DOI 10.1007/978-3-319-45162-6_6

and, when faced with the facts, denied all responsibility. Recently, the two men had had an intense discussion about environmental pollution. One of their plants was producing methane, ammonia, and other toxic substances that were harmful to health and affected air quality. Steve maintained that it was high time something was done about it but Tom would have none of it. He stuck to the position that there was no real scientific evidence for global warming. In the meantime, the company's poor record on environmental issues was widely discussed in the media, causing significant damage to its reputation.

Eventually, Tom's denialism was confronted at a specially convened board meeting. Ostensibly, the reason for the meeting was the IT fiasco, but the bad press the company was receiving as a serious polluter proved to be the tipping point. All board members unanimously resolved to pass a motion of no confidence, giving Tom no alternative but to resign. Afterwards, when asked to comment on what had happened, Tom accused a number of the board members of being part of a cabal that enjoyed character assassination. He had been treated completely unfairly; he was in the right.

We come across denialists everywhere, in all walks of life. According to the *Oxford English Dictionary*, a denialist is "a person who refuses to admit the truth of a concept or proposition that is supported by the majority of scientific or historical evidence." This large group includes creationists (rejection of the theory of evolution); holocaust deniers (there was no policy of Jewish genocide and the extermination camps did not exist); CEOs of cigarette companies (there is no relationship between cigarette smoking and lung cancer); ex-South African President Thabo Mbeki's skepticism about HIV/AIDS treatment (anti-retroviral drugs don't work); the CEOs of many banks (we had no idea rogue trading was going on); the Roman Catholic Church (there have been no pedophiles among our priests); and deniers of climate change (it has nothing to do with human activity).

What compels denialists to stick to specific belief systems or ideas in spite of solid evidence to the contrary? What blinds them to reality? The answer is that they resort to a formidable, ingrained defense mechanism.

Defense mechanisms are complex cognitive/emotive processes that protect our psychological equilibrium from anxiety or conflict and are triggered by upsetting situations. Denial is one of the most common and automatic human defense mechanisms. Short periods of denial can be helpful, in that they give us the mental space to unconsciously process distressing information. But in the long run, denialism becomes hard work and it takes a lot of mental gymnastics to maintain it. This explains not only why people refuse to change their minds when presented with hard evidence that proves them wrong, but also why they do everything in their power to prove themselves right, even to the point of absurdity.

We usually see denialism (of an addiction, mental health issues, relationship problems, etc.) at an individual level but denialism also takes place in a wider societal context. A major cause of denialism on a larger scale is our tendency to subscribe to alternative narratives—ideologies, politics, religious dogma—rather than to what is true. Another cause is the unwillingness to acknowledge shameful events or trauma in a community's history. Examples include the Turkish government's denials of the Armenian genocide under the Ottoman Empire, the Japanese government's disclaimers about the existence of "comfort women" (sex slaves) in World War II, the US government's continued refusal to introduce gun control, and the denial of race issues in a number of societies.

In Tom's case, we could hypothesize that he was trying to protect himself by refusing to accept the truth about what was happening in the company, even after he was fired. He continued to deny his responsibility for the IT disaster, remained an apologist for climate change denial, and blamed the problems in the company on other people and forces beyond his control. His response to his firing revealed two other salient characteristics of denialism: suspicion of others and belief in conspiracies.

How can we deal with denialism when its roots run so deep in the human psyche? How do we identify it? How do we manage and reason with denialists?

At a societal level, magical thinking is hard to change. Sometimes only a serious crisis will shake denialists out of their illusions. The current confrontation over climate change is a case in point. Tackling denialism at an individual level may be simpler and require a less dramatic process than global warming.

The first step is to recognize when this defense mechanism is at work. One clear warning sign is recurring negative experiences, for example, a series of harmful relationships, the side effects of addictive behavior, etc. However, getting denialists to acknowledge these signs may be difficult, as they touch on their sense of identity. Denialism is an adaptive and creative strategy designed to help people maintain their sanity and keep their sense of self and worldview intact. Therefore, when we try to change these cognitive frameworks, we can expect a strong emotional backlash, especially if people do not like the reality we are presenting.

Confronting denialists head on with "facts" may only strengthen their defenses. Instead, we need to roll with the punches. To have a real impact, we may have to engage in a considerable amount of psychological judo. The use of mild, open-ended questions, or nudging reminders about certain facts may set a rethinking process into motion and stimulate a willingness to face unpleasant realities. However, only denialists can take themselves off the path of denial, and this will only happen if they make a deliberate choice of reality.

The best thing to do is to prevent denialism occurring in the first place. It's a good idea to surround ourselves with people who have a different outlook from our own and who will challenge our opinions and assumptions. We should take care not to associate only with like-minded people. We all need a devil's advocate from time to time. It remains debatable, however, whether someone like Tom will ever accept the challenge presented by alternative points of view.

Questions

- Are you quick to believe in conspiracy theories that are intended to suppress the truth?
- Do you often see yourself as the underdog fighting "corrupt" elites that promote sinister agendas?
- Do people accuse you of cherry-picking, using selective information to prove a point? Do they suggest you prefer make-believe to hard facts?

- Are you tempted to put up smokescreens when faced with inconvenient truths?
- In discussions with people who disagree with you, are you prepared to reconsider the sources of information you have been using?
- Are you prepared to reflect on the emotional reasons why you hang on to a particular point of view and to look at the underlying reasons for your strong opinions?

7

It's Hard Being Normal

Mental Health Issues

What is "normal" in mental health terms? Is being normal doing what normal people do? Should we aspire to be normal? Is it normal not to feel normal? Is it normal when we realize that we are different from others?

Normality is a subjective, relative concept: what might seem normal to another person might feel very far from normal to me. Or, conversely, one person's weird might very well be someone else's normal. On the other hand, I once overheard someone saying, "I don't do normal. I have a reputation to uphold." What was she thinking?

Does being normal mean conforming to specific standards of the *Diagnostic and Statistical Manual of the Mental Disorders (DSM-V)*—the psychiatrists' handbook? Is there a statistical norm for normal? Does it mean that every normal person is, in fact, only average? My own observation is quite the opposite. As I have learned from long experience, everybody is normal until you know him or her better. "Normal" often hides the downright odd, if not tragic. We are all a little bit crazy. At times I have found myself thinking that "normal" people are the strangest of us all.

In everyday situations, people judge normality by comparing others to their own implicit benchmark for normal behavior. The thinking goes

M.F.R. Kets de Vries, *Riding the Leadership Rollercoaster*,
DOI 10.1007/978-3-319-45162-6_7

that if being normal is the goal, then you have to know what normal people are supposed to do. But in fact, there is no such thing as normal. Or to put it another way: normal is the messy, inconsistent way we get through life.

Let's look at the conundrum from the other side and ask what is abnormality? Although each of us has an internal sense of what is normal, when we move outside our comfort zone our notion of normal is challenged. What was once normal may suddenly feel, or be perceived as, abnormal. We naturally seek cognitive and emotional alignment between the external world and our internal world. When there is misalignment, most people either try to adapt, or deny to themselves that they feel abnormal. But this self-imposed normalcy can trigger a variety of psychological problems.

Trying to fit into the world of work is no exception. Most people in organizations want to appear normal, particularly senior executives. They are highly visible; they don't want others to see the strange inner life that they may be leading.

Karin, a senior executive had consciously worked throughout her career to fit into the organizations she worked for. And on first impression, she seemed like a normal married person, living a normal life in a normal suburb, working at a normal job. But when night came, things were different. It was as if Karin had two different personas; two people who took turns to share her body. She was like a swan, appearing serene and elegant on the surface, but she felt that underneath the water she was still the ugly duckling, paddling like crazy to maintain the illusion.

To appear normal, Karin struggled to hide her doubts about herself. At work, she wore an Italian couture suit, like the normal private equity banker she was. Her out-of-hours persona, however, was more feral rock chick. She preferred tight jeans, a silk T-shirt, and a leather jacket. She smoked marijuana and spent most of her time in trendy bars in whatever city she happened to be in, picking up men or women. When she unleashed this alter ego, it was as if she was operating in a self-induced, hypnotic state.

Predictably, juggling these two versions of normal made Karin's life very difficult. She felt like a walking contradiction, only one step away from psychological implosion. Both versions overlapped and played out in Karin's inner world. She was a hard-driving banker who was excellent at her job and much of her professional talent was grounded in her edgy, risk-loving side. But she could not admit this, even to herself, and so the two normals that struggled for dominance in Karin's inner world made her feel abnormal everywhere, even though she was good at acting normal.

Her marriage took a hit when her husband discovered a text from a man mentioning a "great night, to be continued." Karin felt guilty but reacted angrily, saying she had no idea who the person was, or what had taken place. Within a week she moved into an apartment on her own. She became depressed and struggled to function in her work. Sensing weakness, her colleagues turned on her and after a harsh performance evaluation, Karin was fired. Late that night, with the business suit she had shed on one side of the bed, and her leather jacket on the other, she was conscious that neither felt right to her any longer. She realized she needed to figure out what was "normal" and "abnormal" for her, and how she could make it all fit. Karin decided to consult a therapist to help her untangle her life.

This turned out to be a long process. It was very painful at times, but also—appealing to Karin's curious, risk-taking persona—exhilarating. She told her therapist: "I am discovering that the most interesting person I have ever met in my life is … me!" Over time Karin crafted a new life by building on what felt normal to her in both personas—work and love. Her dark side fueled a creative energy that she applied to her new job in a smaller investment bank, where she was extremely successful. Being "normal" compared to her work colleagues—most of whom were men—would always be an elusive concept for Karin, but now she was aware that being slightly "different" was in fact an asset. She also started seeing her estranged husband for dinner several times a month. They agreed to work toward friendship, and then take it from there.

Turning back to my initial question—What is "normal"?—the best answer is that we have to figure that out for ourselves. But while there may be no set formula for normal, healthier people do have a common set of characteristics. These include a stable sense of identity, a greater capacity for reality testing, and mature, rather than primitive, defense mechanisms. For example, they take responsibility for their actions rather than blaming others for setbacks. Healthier people are not afraid to experience and explore the full range of human emotions and know how to manage their anxieties. Importantly, they can establish and maintain intimate and sexually satisfying relationships. They accept help and advice. They are creative and playful. And, finally, they are able to reflect on their behavior and how it synchronizes with their values and ideals.

The next question, then, is how to attain this level of mental health? Executive coaches and psychotherapists encourage their clients to reassess their goals and motivations, and evaluate their strengths and weaknesses. They work with the client to identify the causes and triggers of self-destructive behavior. Like Karin, many people find that, with this kind of help, they realize getting to know themselves is more interesting than "acting out" and running away from the things that distress them.

Questions

- What does being "normal" or "abnormal" mean to you?
- Do you like being "normal?" Or for you, does "normal" mean being "average," not special, like everyone else?
- Do you view being "abnormal" as a bad thing? Do you like or prefer to fit in?
- Do you go around with the feeling that there is something wrong with you?
- Are you experiencing situations that impair your functioning in areas of your life (work, home, school environment, or relationships)?
- How good do you think you are at tolerating behavior that differs from your own? What kind of "abnormal" behavior is unacceptable to you?
- Does being "normal" imply feeling that what you are doing or saying is normal to you, or does it mean that what you are doing or saying is normal by society's standards?

8

The M&A Crap Game

"Marrying" to Fight Boredom

Noreen was wondering yet again what had gone wrong. The deal had looked so promising two years ago, so why had everything turned sour? Over and over again she had emphasized that the merger would create substantial value for the customers and shareholders of both companies, contributing to competitive advantage and increased market power. It was a no-brainer. It would be good for everyone. Synergy was the key word.

But now it was time for some honest, if painful, thinking. Noreen could now admit that there had been other unspoken reasons for pressing for the merger. When the very reputable investment bank had approached her about the possibility of making this deal, it had caught her at a vulnerable time. She had been bored rigid with the routine of her work. Entering merger negotiations had made her feel alive again. The consulting firm she brought in also saw the merger as a great opportunity and warned her that if she didn't take the initiative, the other company might move against hers. The idea that she might miss the boat made Noreen anxious. Obviously, it was better to eat than to be eaten. The Pac-Man metaphor—used by an investment banker—still resonated.

M.F.R. Kets de Vries, *Riding the Leadership Rollercoaster*,
DOI 10.1007/978-3-319-45162-6_8

Nothing about the process had been easy. The other company was determined to remain independent, knowing that there is no such a thing as a merger of equals. She knew that most mergers are thinly veiled takeovers. Closing the deal required a considerable amount of arm-twisting and lots of money. But after it was done, Noreen was very proud of the fact that the merger had created by far the biggest company in its field.

However, the promised synergies never materialized. The consulting firm's analytics proved to be unrealistic and many of their assumptions flawed. The efficiencies from the expected economies of scale and scope remained elusive. With hindsight, Noreen realized that she had had no idea what she was up against. Closing the deal was the easiest part of the equation; making the merger work was the really difficult part. With no transition plan to enable rapid action after the merger, she had been unprepared for the challenges of the culture integration process.

It became crystal clear to Noreen that the synergy expected from the merger had been wildly overestimated. There had been far too much hyperbole and projection and not enough considered reflection. Of course, there had been some savings, as downsizing had been the order of the day. However, a recent survey had shown that morale in the company was at an all-time low.

Of course, not everyone had been unhappy. A number of people had benefited greatly from the merger, including the investment bank, the consulting firm, and the lawyers. But Noreen realized that their agenda had been quite different from hers. Obviously, their interests lay in the short term: the financial gains of closing the deal, and not whether it would work afterwards. And she couldn't deny that she hadn't done too badly herself, given the lucrative financial package she had received when the merger was completed. The same could be said about the outgoing CEO of the other company. Yet the share price was at an all-time low. The shareholders were restless. They had started to accuse her of making a poor financial deal. It made her very nervous about her own job security. Looking back, Noreen wondered, was the merger really worth it?

Noreen has good reason to worry. It's estimated that 50–80% of mergers do not produce any increase in shareholder value. Time after time, it has been shown that the majority of mergers are plain failures.

And mega-deals, in particular, are the most likely to fail. Too often a merger transforms two tottering companies into one larger tottering one. Although most deals look great on paper, in the excitement of making a deal people forget the difficulties that will follow. Given these dismal statistics (which turn mergers into some kind of crap game) you have to ask why these deals are even made at all?

One key explanation for entering the M&A game is greed. There will always be people who are out to make short-term gains from such deals. After the merger, they can continue to make money through spin-offs, split-ups, and liquidations. People with this mindset are not bothered by the fact that synergy may just be another word for cost-cutting through "de-hiring." The personal and social costs that these practices entail are the least of their worries.

Furthermore, mergers are considered a more attractive alternative than having to reinvent an antiquated business model. Making deals is the fastest way for companies to compensate for their failure to grow organically. Another common but untold story behind mergers has to do with ego and boredom: who doesn't want to be the biggest kid on the block? And the day-to-day routine of work can be boring. Noreen was certainly no stranger to both susceptibilities.

Given that M&As will continue to be made despite these dismal statistics, what can be done to increase the odds of success? Are there specific practices and processes that can make mergers more successful?

Research has shown that mergers between companies operating in the same industry do better. Also, the chance of a successful M&A will also be higher where the parties have previous merger experience. It goes without saying that friendly (as opposed to hostile) mergers will have a greater chance of success. Unlike what happened in Noreen's case, the executive teams of both companies have to buy into and support the merger.

It's also important to understand the financials. Will the merger benefit all parties involved? Will it make them a stronger, more competitive player in the market? And beyond financials, soft data need attention. Is there an authentic strategic fit? Has there been any cultural auditing? What identity challenges might arise out of the merger? How will perceived "winners" and "losers" be managed? And are there sufficient resources in place to manage these processes?

Making a merger succeed requires a lot of trust between the merging parties. If both parties express a willingness to merge, a well-formulated common vision will go a long way to make a merger successful. This should be a vision shared by both companies to build something that is not just bigger but also better. Success is also likelier if both companies have complementary histories and compatible corporate cultures. It helps when both companies speak the same language (literally and figuratively) and have understanding and respect for each other's leadership philosophy.

Once the decision to merge has been made, the main focus should be on a rapid integration process. From my experience, speed matters. The longer uncertainty drags on, the greater the level of anxiety among employees. Tough decisions should be made fairly and swiftly. Once again, trust—something that was missing in Noreen's case—will be a factor in resolving difficult issues. It's essential that the company perceived as the "loser" in the merger game should be able to keep its dignity. This means fair process in the allocation of senior executive positions is a must, as are attractive incentives for key executives to remain.

I have found it helpful in the case of an M&A to put together some kind of senior executive SWAT team that includes key players of both companies. This team will be responsible for deploying transition teams to familiarize and engage employees in the M&A process through transition/integration workshops that lay out the rationale behind the merger—the "dream" of the future company, a common identity, the "rules of the game," performance objectives, reward structure, and the planned timetable. While these integration activities take place throughout the organization, senior managers need to be seen to set an example and walk the walk and talk the talk. Their behavior must be aligned with the vision and values of the new organization that is being formed.

The merger of two companies has been described as the financial equivalent of the decision of two people to have a baby to save a marriage. But as is so often the case in those marriages, making a new company may not be the answer. Most merger deals, even those that look fantastic on paper (and most do), stumble when the real work starts. Only in situations where there is a great amount of trust, cultural compatibility, and discretionary management resources, will mergers have a chance to thrive. As Noreen's case illustrates, too often acquirers have to cope with an acute lack of information and foresight to help them assess possible synergies. The moral of Noreen's story is that the promises made by deal-makers need a great deal of scrutiny before a merger decision is made. And as so few of these deals really work out, it's wise to think twice, then think again, before considering one.

Questions

- How good has your organization been with respect to organic growth? Does your organization have a rather antiquated business model? Is there enough innovation in your organization? If not, is this a cause for worry? Is your organization threatened with takeover?
- As a senior executive, do you feel you are doing more of the same? Are you on automatic pilot? Are you bored?
- Are you being tempted by investment banks and consultants to make deals? Does this make you anxious?
- How far do you consider cultural compatibility when looking at possible candidates for a merger or acquisition?
- How do you plan to allocate the top jobs following an M&A? Would you have concerns at being party to the "conqueror" syndrome, favoring your own executives?
- Have you thought through the ramifications of the post-merger process? Do you plan to have a transition team to facilitate the integration?
- What is your communication strategy—your vision for the integrated company—and your time frame for the change process?
- How do you plan to address people's main fear—of whether they will still have a job post-merger?

9

Team or Harem?

The Me, Me, Me Leader

Edward was thoroughly angry at the situation he found himself in. In fact he was kicking himself. He had plenty of management experience but he'd been so flattered to be asked to join the executive team of the Serail Corporation as VP Finance that he hadn't done his homework properly. He'd just found out that one of his close colleagues had been given an almost identical portfolio.

Naturally, Edward raised the matter with the CEO, who was untroubled: there might be some overlap but their areas of responsibility were different. That was little consolation to Edward, who started to take a much closer look at the other members of the executive team. And he soon discovered that he was not the only one without a clear mandate for their role in the organization. He was also bothered by the number of people reporting directly to the CEO. Edward knew that when teams reach double-digit figures they are cumbersome rather than productive. Things did not look good.

Executive team meetings added to his alarm. They involved little or no discussion and were more like information sessions. Although the team was supposed to be a decision-making body, it was actually constipated, underperforming, and floundering. Edward's colleagues might

M.F.R. Kets de Vries, *Riding the Leadership Rollercoaster*,
DOI 10.1007/978-3-319-45162-6_9

be physically present but they seemed mentally absent. The CEO did most of the talking and everyone else merely echoed what he said, if they said anything at all. Very little got done during these meetings—but that didn't mean that nothing was going on.

Edward knew a fair bit about teams and it now crossed his mind that anyone who knew something about group dynamics would have a field day with Serail's executive group. Most of its members had devised highly creative ways to avoid dealing with the real issues, resorting to veiled, guarded, or sniping comments. The allocation of resources was a perennial agenda item. The question of who was going to get what dominated every meeting and explained the highly politicized atmosphere. Everyone was competing for the CEO's attention and all their energy was going into making the CEO feel good. It came as no surprise to Edward that most of the decisions made were sub-optimal.

However, he was amazed that in spite of the team's obvious dysfunctionality nobody (including him) was leaving. Why not? Was it because they were all so well paid? Were they all held back by their golden handcuffs? When that image came to Edward's mind, it reminded him of something.

A few years previously, Edward had visited the sultan's harem in the Topkapi Palace in Istanbul and he remembered now that it had been described as a "golden cage"—the women lived in such luxury that even if they had been able to leave, few of them would have chosen to. They were undeniably captives and they knew it but they also had the ear of the sultan and were potentially in positions of great power. Edward had a small epiphany: the CEO was the sultan and he and his fellow executive team members were his harem. All this jockeying for favors paralleled the political maneuvering in the sultan's harem.

The more he thought about it, the more Edward was convinced he had identified the key theme of the CEO's leadership style. He was the sultan of Serail Corporation. Why should he get rid of people if they were still of some use? A harem of executives meant that he always had reserves to hand in case anyone got too fed up and left. They all liked having their boss's ear and he was sure that the information he needed would flow up to him. In fact, given the way he had structured communication, he had become irreplaceable as team leader. By keeping other members' positions insecure and ambiguous, he could ensure they would all vie for his attention. He controlled them all. Everyone in the company was at his beck and call.

But what about the CEO's professed enthusiasm for teamwork? Not a week went by without his recommending a book or article about the organizational advantages of team working. He was evangelistic about it. Edward realized it was just lip service paid to an idea. Maybe the CEO was kidding himself? Either way, what his boss really preferred was playing sultan to his executive harem. Meanwhile the company was starting to feel the cost of this idiosyncratic organizational design. Most team meetings were a complete waste of time, although nobody had the courage to say so, and team members' feelings of alienation and disengagement were increasing.

From a leader's perspective, there are some advantages to running an organization through a harem system. As a social structure, harems suit alpha males perfectly. Historically, a harem allowed a ruler access to numerous fertile and available women. In return, the women enjoyed a high degree of comfort and protection. And of course, there were often opportunities for a powerful woman to rule from behind the sultan's throne.

However, there are downsides to harems for everyone involved. Harem leaders need to be permanently on their guard against others who would like to usurp their power. And, as Edward had noticed, fierce intra-harem competition for resources leads to a great waste of energy. At Serail this had made decision-making extremely laborious and implementation unpredictable and slow. Harems are also very expensive to maintain; duplicated responsibilities mean duplicated salaries and at Serail the salaries were sufficiently generous to stop most people questioning their situation. So why had the CEO set up such a structure in the first place?

In my experience, leaders who prefer harem-style management systems are prone to narcissistic dysfunctionality. Although they may come across as charming, the reality is very different. They manipulate and exploit others for their own benefit. Potential members had better beware they are not signing up for the golden cage and ask themselves, team or harem?

Narcissistic leaders want blind, unquestioning obedience from everyone who works for them as well as a great deal of admiration. They have to be the center of attention and treated as special. Their sense of entitlement means they can be arrogant and haughty, treating others with contempt and arrogance. They will be the dominant force in any conversation, believing that they have the answers to most problems. Hand in hand with their neediness is their hypersensitivity to how they are perceived by others. Anyone who dares to criticize or question their behavior quickly becomes the "enemy."

At Serail, things were regressing rather than progressing and Edward wondered whether it was really worth hanging on to his position in his boss's harem. The privilege came at too high a price. At times, the CEO threw him crumbs of attention, making flattering suggestions that he had a great future in the company. But Edward's flash of insight now made him feel that his boss was keeping him and the other members of the executive team in a state of bondage. And if their influence was so weak, who did have the CEO's ear? Was there some shadowy figure behind the CEO's throne?

Teams are not always the answer to every problem or to creating high-performance organizations. Far too much can be made of them. A substantial body of research has shown many of the claims made about the benefits of teamwork are fantasy rather than reality. There are too many teams that soak up time and resources and a dysfunctional team can create a toxic environment throughout an organization.

It can also be an uphill struggle to transform a collection of individuals with different personalities and into an integrated and effective work unit. It's difficult enough finding team players; getting them to play together is even more of a challenge.

Far too often, teams are created just because they seem to be a good thing to have. This kind of gesture management means teams have no clear goals or measures of success, fuzzy boundaries, and poorly defined roles and tasks. If the members of a team do not have a clear mandate for what needs to be done, form takes precedence over substance, and empty rhetoric over real work. What is the point of building a team, if good people are put into bad systems, as they were at Serail? If you find yourself on a team with a harem style of leadership, you should think hard about whether you'd really like to stay.

Of course, when teams work well the advantages far outweigh the disadvantages. An effective team can energize an entire organization, contribute to a learning, collaborative culture, stimulate creativity and innovation, and make its members more productive. A real team can be a very powerful force. But pseudo teams, like the Serail harem, with a "me, me, me" leader, will simply bleed resources, stifle talent, and encourage infighting.

Questions

- On a scale of 1 to 10 (1 = lowest, 10 = highest) how do you rate the team you are part of?
- If your score is low, can you explain why your team is not functioning very well? Is it a team in name only? Why?
- What steps need to be taken to improve the score you have given to the team?
- Does the person in charge of the team seem to prefer dealing with people on a one-to-one basis? If so, can you explain why?
- Do you believe that the person in charge of the team is really getting the best out of team members?
- What can you say about your team leader's leadership style? How would you describe it?

10

OK, That's It

Retirement

When Jerry came to see me, he complained of feelings of deep sadness and emptiness. He felt lost in his life. He and his wife were more like strangers sharing a space than two people with anything in common. Their children, now grown up, were all busy building lives of their own and he seemed unable to find a way to relate to them, their interests, and their young families. He thought endlessly about the emptiness of his life, which had formerly seemed so full and rewarding. When I asked him about his own interests, it was clear he had never had any outside work. He was very depressed. There was a sense of helplessness and hopelessness about him. He also seemed physically unwell. In his case—as is true for many people—retirement has a detrimental effect on his health. Jerry was a recently retired CEO.

For people like Jerry, the public recognition that accompanies a position at the top of an organization becomes the most meaningful dimension of their lives. Their life anchors are their identification with an institution of great power; influence over individuals, policies, finances, and the community; and constant affirmation of their importance as individuals and their role as a leader.

M.F.R. Kets de Vries, *Riding the Leadership Rollercoaster*,
DOI 10.1007/978-3-319-45162-6_10

With retirement, all these anchors disappear overnight. The destabilizing effect is often exacerbated by a realization of what has been lost, or sacrificed, over the years earlier, on the way to the top—a personal life, good relationships with spouse, children, and friends, and time to develop outside contacts and interests. This is one reason why many top executives delay retiring and cling to power for as long as they can.

Other hidden but potent psychological and emotional factors also conspire to make retirement difficult. To begin with, people usually attain top leadership positions just when the effects of aging become more noticeable. When the face frowning back at us from the mirror starts to show the inevitable effects of time, a wave of negative emotions is released: fear, anxiety, grief, depression, and anger.

Self-consciousness about physical deterioration (a sense of being not as good as we used to be) can stimulate a search for substitutes for attractiveness and virility. For some—especially top executives in prestigious positions—wielding power is an effective substitute for lost looks, an expanding waistline, and having to give up contact sports. As US Secretary of State Henry Kissinger once memorably put it, "Power is the ultimate aphrodisiac." For many executives, power comes with dignity and respect. Small wonder that so many are reluctant to let go of it. If the power of office is the only thing people have left, they will hold onto that office for as long as possible.

Another complicating factor for those faced with the prospect of relinquishing power is the talion principle, or "an eye for an eye," as it is probably better known. This rudimentary system of justice decreed that criminals should receive like-for-like punishment for injuries inflicted on their victims: "be done by as you did." Leadership involves making difficult decisions that affect the lives and happiness of others—both positively and negatively. Unconsciously, leaders file all these decisions in a memory bank and, as the number of their "victims" mounts, so does a sense of anticipated retaliation. This makes them extremely defensive and is yet another incentive to postpone retirement.

It's inevitable that top executives who have placed work at the center of their entire adult lives are devastated when power dynamics shift and a named (but not yet in office) successor begins to win converts to a very different dream for the future of the organization. Like an old lion they will lash out in an attempt to put ambitious ladder-climbers in their place. The wit who said the primary task of a CEO is to find his or her likely successor and kill the bastard had a point: the "bastard" stands to destroy the outgoing CEO's most cherished dreams.

These fears are accentuated by the need we all have to leave a legacy: leaving a reminder of one's accomplishments is a symbolic and defiant gesture toward defeating death. Many top executives question whether their successors can be trusted to respect the edifice that took them so long to build.

Of course, for some, retirement raises financial questions. They will no longer have the financial resources to continue their way of life. They worry that they will need to make dramatic cuts in their living standard.

Unhappily, most companies fail woefully to understand the psychological dynamics of retirement. The default mode is to give people on the verge of retirement little or no help to prepare for such a critical life change. It is exasperating that so few recognize the opportunity that helping executives transition to retirement can represent for the organization as well as the individual concerned. No one can stop executives from aging, but companies can certainly put a far more positive spin on retirement procedures.

Some companies get it right, however. The case of Ronald, former head of Asia in a global information technology firm, illustrates how it can be done. In this company, the VP for talent management had been eager to create special work arrangements for hard-to-replace, experienced executives approaching the mandatory retirement age.

With the support of the group CEO, she introduced a flexible, phased retirement policy that allowed senior executives approaching normal retirement age to reduce the hours they worked, or work for the organization in a different capacity after retirement. This gave retirees the opportunity to transition gradually, in contrast to the abrupt termination common in many companies, and meant that the company would not lose their knowledge and experience in one blow.

Ronald became a special advisor to the group CEO with a brief to help develop the company's African markets. The arrangement not only helped the CEO to develop a strategy and organization for a fast-growing region, it also gave Ronald and his wife space to experiment with non-workplace activities without his having to leave the workplace altogether. In fact, both had always had a special interest in Africa, making Ronald's continuing work something both could engage in.

Arrangements like Ronald's are win-win situations for both companies and retirees. Given the damage that can be caused by a powerful executive's struggle to retain power and remain relevant, managing slow retirements could be at least as important as bringing new hires on board swiftly.

The question remains, how can people like Jerry, who see retirement as a statement of personal as well as professional redundancy, be helped? How will it be possible to enable them to see retirement in terms of opportunity, rather than as an approach to death?

Jerry's case is genuinely worrying. Mortality appears to be higher among executives who retire earlier than those who decide to continue working. Of course, a factor in Jerry's situation is that he really loved his job. Given Jerry's personality, it will be important for him to find ways to continue leading an active, meaningful life. People who are happiest in retirement deal with the question of meaning by "giving back" and rediscovering a sense of purpose.

Questions

- What steps have you taken to prepare for your retirement?
- What does life after retirement mean to you? What fantasies do you have about your life after retirement? How do you plan to spend your time?
- Do you have a life outside work?
- Do you believe that retirement is going to be beneficial or detrimental to your health?
- What activities give you most pleasure? What kinds of routines are most important to you?
- If you no longer had your job, what would you miss most?
- Does your organization offer the possibility of phased retirement?

11

What, Already? Meeting the Grim Reaper

I'm willing to bet that death rarely features in discussions in the boardroom or around the water cooler. It certainly doesn't feature in mainstream motivational theories or textbooks on organizational behavior and motivation. But death is out there, an alarming and ever-present reality, and it affects every aspect of our life, including work, whether or not we talk or think about it. Because death is the ultimate stealth motivator.

When I met Victor, the VP Purchasing of a large automotive parts company, he came across as very successful but also very troubled. He described having panic attacks, expressed concerns about his heart, and complained about feeling generally unwell. His manic pace at work could be interpreted as a distraction, but (according to Victor) his anxiety about his health was adversely affecting the quality of his work. He felt that if he continued as he was, he would burn out and have a breakdown. Victor was convinced that something was wrong with him but he couldn't put his finger on what it was.

Victor told me at length about the many doctors he had visited. In spite of all the tests he had been subjected to, they didn't seem to find anything wrong with him. He found this difficult to accept. He said forcefully that there had to be something more. Something physical must

M.F.R. Kets de Vries, *Riding the Leadership Rollercoaster*,
DOI 10.1007/978-3-319-45162-6_11

be causing his panic attacks. He worried that he had a disease that wasn't so easy to diagnose—some obscure cancer, multiple sclerosis, Lyme disease, even a brain tumor.

People like Victor, who suffer from panic attacks, are inclined to convince themselves that they suffer from a broad range of health problems. In many instances, their hypochondriacal concerns are related to a fear of death. Death anxiety seems to be highly correlated with hypochondriasis. Fear of death features largely in somatic and related disorders, characterized by multiple visits to doctors, and requests for medical tests to identify what turn out to be illusory health problems.

Of course, every time someone we know dies, we are reminded, even if only subliminally, that death is an intricate part of life, something that many of us find difficult to accept. The fear of death is a significant and omnipresent source of anxiety that impacts our social, personal, spiritual, and physical existence. Death anxiety is a basic fear underlying our development, maintenance, and numerous psychological conditions.

To cope with this lingering concern, we "outsource" death. We try to neutralize it. In our late twenties and early thirties we work frenetically to get ahead, not recognizing that life is finite. By our forties we start to become more aware of the time left to live as people close to us start to get sick and die. Eventually a great part of what we do is intricately tied to death. Yet still the subject remains taboo.

While some respond to the fear of death by refusing to get out of bed and pulling the bedclothes over their head, the more usual response is quite the opposite. In most cases people push all thoughts of death to the back of their minds while running their lives and businesses at a frantic pace. Whether people harness this activity in a positive way or run around like a rat in a maze is an indication of how well they address fears of their inevitable end.

Intellectually there is no denying death awaits us all, but truly acknowledging it is a very different thing. When we repress our fear of death we can develop a conscious or unconscious death anxiety. I am suggesting that death anxiety underlies a great deal of executive behavior and action and as it intensifies, there are three common maladaptive responses that affect the work environment.

The first is the manic defense—workaholism. For some executives, work becomes an immortality system. Typically, workaholics use incessant activity as a way to avoid depressive thoughts and push away lingering subconscious fears of death. Unfortunately, in contemporary organizations workaholism is encouraged, supported, and well compensated. But a workaholic environment can contribute to serious organizational problems, including low morale, depression, substance abuse, workplace harassment, above-average rates of absenteeism, and burnout. I once knew an executive so driven by anxiety that he took his company on an acquisition spree that he was unable to stop. It may have been a way to help him feel alive but it ultimately affected his company's economic viability.

Another response to death anxiety is a refusal to deal with succession issues. Many senior executives determinedly resist dealing with the big question of "life after me" because it is too anxiety provoking. Meanwhile the organization suffers and stagnates and productivity stalls because of the leader's failure to let go.

The third response is the attempt to evade mortality by creating a tangible legacy—an organization, building, award, or similar, that will preserve someone's name or memory. The "edifice complex" seems to be alive and well. There are innumerable examples, from the pyramids of Ancient Egypt, through to the Taj Mahal, and Nicolae Ceauşescu's absurdly huge and still unfinished Palace of the Parliament in Bucharest, only one-third of which is ever used and which costs as much to heat and light as a city the size of Baltimore. There is a psychological parallel between making a mark on the landscape with a building and the exercise of power. Creating a business that will be continued by family members is another obvious way of ensuring some form of immortality. This conscious or subconscious wish lies at the core of many family business dynasties.

However, keeping busy and building a legacy do not have to be dysfunctional activities. When we can be sure there is meaning to our work, life has significance and death anxiety can be eased.

Being able to work at something that has meaning is very important. By creating meaning for themselves and others in the workplace, executives can alleviate the feelings of uselessness that both feed off and heighten death anxiety. All of us like to know what we do can help make the world a better place for the next generation.

Building meaning, rather than structures, could be another way of leaving a legacy. This wide brief could include many things, from rebuilding relationships with the next generation—the most important legacy—or creating a program or foundation that will continue to help people after its initiator is gone.

Humans are said to be unique in that we adapt and run our lives in the full knowledge not only of our beginning but also of our inevitable ending. But our anxiety about death causes a great degree of conscious or unconscious discomfort that manifests itself in a wide variety of affective, cognitive, developmental, and sociocultural reactions. How we metabolize our anxiety about death determines whether we experience work as meaningful or meaningless. Unresolved death anxiety can result in heightened stress and even psychological burnout.

Death anxiety is something everyone should be aware of. It can be dealt with by getting people to confront and talk about their fear and by creating an environment where people feel their work has lasting relevance and significance. Ultimately many executives (and people in general) are more afraid of a meaningless existence than death itself.

So, how to help Victor? In our interactions I tried to help him understand that physical pain, psychological distress, and existential suffering are part of the human condition. To find a way of coping with his feelings of anxiety, I emphasized the importance of meaning and purpose in his life, the need for social support—building meaningful relationships. These discussions proved helpful in reducing his maladaptive coping mechanisms, resolving unconscious and conscious conflicts, and helping him recognize depressive symptoms and possible triggers, eventually contributing to a change in his dysfunctional behavior patterns. By improving his self-esteem, meaning, and relatedness, Victor was able to strengthen his anxiety-buffering system, becoming less stressed, less driven, and feeling more in control of his life.

Questions

- Do you worry much about your health and dying?
- Are you preoccupied with death and avoiding death, to the point where it is all you think about?

- Are you going to the doctor often but finding that there is nothing wrong with you? Do you believe that doctors don't appreciate that you may have health problems?
- Do you have panic attacks without obvious reasons?
- Do you rarely feel good about yourself? Do you fear burnout?
- Is it hard for you to relax?
- Does your mood sag when you don't have a specific task to work on?
- Are you concerned about life's meaning and purpose? Are you prepared to talk about these issues?

Part II

Going Up …

12

You've Got to Laugh
Humor in the Workplace

Everyone agreed that Jack, the company's VP Information Systems, was a very funny guy. He had an unusual way with humor; self-deprecating, he knew how to get laughs out of people and to help them see the lighter side of things. But there was also a darker side to his humor, especially when it was directed at others. Some laughed when he joked about others' imperfections, but found his words left them with a bitter aftertaste. His co-workers began to feel unsure about the way Jack used humor. He gave off conflicting signals. Was he using humor as a defense against his own insecurities? Was his self-deprecation covering up real fear and pain? Was his teasing of others a mask for his underlying hostility? Or was making others the butt of his jokes a way of deflecting attention from himself and avoiding getting too close to them?

Humor is a complex cognitive function that often, but not necessarily, leads to laughter. It may be used in numerous ways, to both a positive and negative effect. It has often been said that there is a thin line between comedy and tragedy, humor and hurt. Most of us engage in humor to entertain. Laughing with others is congenial and empathetic: it brings people together. Humor is also a great way to relieve psychological tensions. It puts us face-to-face with life's incongruities; the disparity

M.F.R. Kets de Vries, *Riding the Leadership Rollercoaster*,
DOI 10.1007/978-3-319-45162-6_12

between what we expect and what we experience can be absurd and therefore comical. Humor can also help us to deal with situations that are beyond our control or depressing. It can provide an optimistic perspective or a temporary light at the end of the tunnel. But humor can also be used maliciously. Laughing at someone else may be funny for some but not for the person who is the subject of the ridicule. In those cases it's easy to see how humor can lead to resentment.

From an evolutionary perspective, humor must have a survival value, like all the characteristics that have been passed on through natural selection. Humor makes us feel better and is good for our mental health. Humor that leads to laughter has a positive effect on our emotional and physical health. Shared laughter helps us to connect to other people and encourages social activities. By turning negatives into positives, generating optimism and creating hope in face of despair, humor can help us cope with the challenges of life. Our human need for humor explains why some people can make a living out of making people laugh but it takes a natural comic genius to reply, as the legendary Bob Hope did when asked on his deathbed where he would like to be buried, "Surprise me."

Of course, we cannot all be Bob Hope but we can all nurture our sense of humor. From a physiological perspective, research has shown that laughter gives our bodies a positive workout and has a stress-reducing effect. People who resort to humor in the situations of stress are more resilient. Functional magnetic resonance imaging (fMRI) scans have shown that humor and laughter change the biochemistry of our brain and hormone system. The use of humor, in stressful situations, slows our heart rate, lowers blood pressure, and eases muscle tension, affecting our levels of epinephrine, norepinephrine, and cortisol. Humor helps to boost infection-fighting antibodies and has a positive effect on our immune system. It's little wonder that people who use humor are more likely to be healthier and to live longer—in Bob Hope's case, to 100.

From a psychological perspective, the complex nature of humor means that it is not merely fun and games. There is much more to humor than we may be consciously aware of. In his study, *Jokes and Their Relation to the Unconscious*, Sigmund Freud noted that humor was a significant defense mechanism to release repressed sexual and aggressive tensions—but also one of the healthier ways of navigating through the conflict and the vicissitudes of life. His daughter, Anna Freud (who built on his work), pointed out that defense mechanisms can be healthy or unhealthy, depending on the circumstance and people who use them. While some defensive strategies are extremely dysfunctional, contributing to maladaptive behavior that may threaten the mental health of the person, others can help us live happy, productive lives. We can even classify defense mechanisms into a hierarchy of severity ranging from pathological, to immature, to neurotic, to mature. Not surprisingly, humor fits into the last category.

Humor also serves a functional and social purpose. It is an age-old device to express criticism about injustices, arrogance, pretentions, or hypocrisies that can't socially (or legally) be expressed in other forms. Humor can be a foray into "taboo" or "politically incorrect" issues and subjects. One of the earliest historical figures to be firmly associated with humor and laughter was the Greek philosopher Democritus, also known as the "laughing philosopher" because of his tendency to mock his fellow citizens and general human folly. In many of Shakespeare's plays, the fool is often paradoxically the wisest and most honest character, speaking truth to power. And in the twentieth-century landscape, comedians and satirists like Charlie Chaplin, John Cleese, and Woody Allen cloaked biting criticism in enduring funny entertainment. Humor is a way of making the unbearable bearable and the unspeakable known.

Humor can, however, have a negative and alienating effect. Sarcastic or derisive humor—making others the butt of jokes—is often contemptuous, hostile, and manipulative. Sarcasm reveals more about the attacker than the person under attack. Derived from the Greek word "*sarkazein*," which means "to tear the flesh off," sarcasm is really thinly disguised hostility masquerading as humor. In contrast, self-deprecating humor is disarming and inclusive. It means amusing others at our own expense and suggests humility on the part of the humorist. A wide range of possibilities lies between these two extremes of humor but whatever form we use or enjoy it would be well to bear in mind that, like most good things in life: everything in moderation. Using humor to excess may suggest underlying feelings of self-doubt, low self-esteem, and other types of anxieties.

Which brings us back to Jack and the confusion he created among his colleagues. Jack was brought up short when he participated in a series of leadership coaching sessions at the company. A 360° feedback assessment report on his leadership strengths and weaknesses revealed that although he used humor to good effect most of the time, it also had unexpected, negative consequences. It was clear from his observers' feedback that Jack needed to do something about his communication style.

Highly surprised by the report, Jack decided to enlist the help of an executive coach. He explained that he had always thought that he used humor in an innocuous way. He meant no harm. He always assumed people would understand what he was trying to say. In response, the coach pointed out that having a good sense of humor is a blessing. But it might be helpful if Jack become conscious of the message he was giving. He used humor to both connect and alienate, which often resulted in crossed signals. The coach pointed out that he did the same in their sessions together: it was often not clear whether Jack was being serious or not, which created a sense of confusion. Jack asked the coach to point out this pattern whenever he did it so that he could deal with it there and then. He explained that he wasn't consciously aware of how compulsive and at times dysfunctional his joking behavior had become.

Exploring the issue more deeply with his coach, Jack realized that he was using humor as a distancing device—as a way to deal with his insecurities and to avoid dealing with conflicting situations. He began to relate this pattern of behavior to his earlier experiences. He had had a difficult and confusing upbringing, growing up in a household where his parents fought daily. Humor had become his survival strategy, a coping mechanism that turned out to be highly effective in defusing the parental quarrels at home. His reliance on humor was reinforced by his experiences at school. Overweight and not good at sports, Jack had been the butt of jokes by many of the other children in his class. His defense against this bullying was to take on the role of class clown. Turning every stressful life event into a joke became Jack's default mode of coping with his personal issues. But (as the feedback report showed) it had turned into a dysfunctional, overused habit at the workplace and one that he needed to break.

With the help of his coach, Jack began to leverage humor as an asset and to use it more constructively. He was able to recognize when humor was appropriate and advantageous—when he could, with others, make fun of the paradoxes and follies that are part of life—and to distinguish situations when its use would be repellent and divisive.

Questions

- Do you often use humor? If so, do you know why?
- Can you reflect on the way you use humor? Is your humor self-deprecatory or sarcastic?
- How do others react to your humorous interventions?
- How do you react to the humor of others?
- Are you often the butt of people's jokes? Do you have any idea why? Why do others pick on you?
- If you are the butt of jokes, how do you "defend" yourself?

13

I Forgive You All

On Forgiveness

In one of my recent leadership development seminars I had a CEO, let's call him Gary, who seemed very bitter about life. He would put a negative spin on every suggestion I made. Curious about his remarkable negativity, I asked him to tell me more about himself. After a little prompting, he was ready to talk—and his narrative wasn't pleasant to hear.

Clearly, I was dealing with a person who bore grudges and was hanging on to grievances that should have been forgiven long ago. He blamed every negative experience he had had, and his current unhappiness, on others. He was not prepared to look at himself and take personal responsibility for his part in the conflicts or events he recounted.

Mahatma Gandhi once said, "An eye for an eye makes the whole world blind." The truth of this comment is especially relevant for people in leadership positions, whose attitudes, beliefs, and behavior have such an important effect on other people's lives. A leader's failure or refusal to forgive can create a climate in which anger, bitterness, and animosity prevent a team, organization, society, or even a whole nation from being the best it can be.

M.F.R. Kets de Vries, *Riding the Leadership Rollercoaster*,
DOI 10.1007/978-3-319-45162-6_13

Of course, all our relationships with others—friends, strangers, or family members—come with the risk of being hurt: like Gary, our parents may have been tough on us, our teachers may have been unpleasant, colleagues at work may have sabotaged our projects, or our friends or partner may have let us down. Any time we let others come close to us, we become vulnerable. And the most logical reaction to an insult or injury is to get even.

In a leadership position, these risks are magnified. Leading others means dealing with a maelstrom of relationships, implying an enormous amount of emotional management. Leaders operate in settings rife with strife that, if left unresolved, can become a festering drag on an organization's effectiveness. People who cannot forgive get stuck into a downward spiral of negativity, taking everyone else down with them.

Good leaders are aware of how costly it is to hold on to grudges and how an unforgiving attitude keeps people from moving forward. Unfortunately, for far too many people in leadership positions, revenge comes more naturally than forgiveness. We have an innate sense of justice: we want others to be punished for what they have done to us. A strong reaction to fairness or unfairness seems to be programmed into our brain, making us hard-wired to retaliate and seek justice when others hurt us.

From an evolutionary point of view, this behavior served a critical purpose. Tit for tat is a way of protecting ourselves. Reciprocity and vengeance are warning signals to violators not to cross that boundary again, or risk escalation and more negative consequences. But they can also open a Pandora's box of counter-reactions: revenge breeds revenge, which can be damaging to our mental and physical health. When we cannot forgive the people who have hurt us, our feelings become a mental poison that destroys our defense system from within. Numerous studies have shown that hatred, spite, bitterness, and vindictiveness are a fertile ground for stress disorders, negatively affecting our immune system. An unforgiving attitude is also positively correlated to depression, anxiety, hostility, and neurosis, and associated with premature death.

But why are some people more inclined to forgive than others and what differentiates them from people who become vindictive and bitter? Taking a psychodynamic-systemic orientation to the study of leaders, I have found three features associated with resistance to forgiving.

The first is obsessional rumination. Unforgiving people spend their time obsessing about their past. People subjected to rigid, autocratic parenting and childhood abuse seem to be more likely to do this, compared to those fortunate enough to grow up in a more benign and nurturing environment.

The second is lack of empathy. Empathy is the evolutionary mechanism that motivates altruistic and pro-social behavior. Imagining and feeling what another person experiences—putting ourselves in the other person's proverbial shoes—allows us to consider the motivations of the transgressor, giving us a route to forgiveness. It is a skill that we learn early on. Children brought up by largely absent or abusive parents generally will find it hard to develop this ability and forgiveness becomes extremely difficult for them.

The third feature is the sense of deprivation. People who had insufficient attention and care as children often focus on what they don't have, and how they can get it. But when they get it, they continue to compare themselves to others, envying their success, reputation, possessions, or personal qualities, often expressing this envy in emotional explosiveness and outbursts of rage.

I would not go so far as to say that people who exhibit these behaviors—and are less likely to forgive—couldn't be leaders. But they will not be the kinds of leaders who get the best out of their followers. The ability to forgive is an essential capability for any leader who wants to make a difference. Of course, forgiveness doesn't mean excusing unacceptable behavior; it is about healing the memory of the harm, not erasing it. When we forgive, we don't change the past, but we can change the future by taking control of our destructive feelings instead of letting them control us, and creating a new way of remembering. Transformational leaders such as Mahatma Gandhi, Nelson Mandela, and Aung San Suu Kyi have figured this out, refusing to replay past hurts and choosing serenity and happiness over righteous anger.

It was not easy for Gary to change his outlook on the world. But as the other participants in the leadership development seminar pointed out, going over and over the same negative feelings was a waste of his time and very unproductive. They emphasized that his unforgiving attitude toward mistakes made by others was not only stressful to him but also very costly to his company. As one of his fellow participants said, "People who don't make mistakes don't do anything!" Practicing forgiveness would be one way to move on.

Other participants pointed out that forgiveness didn't mean that Gary was weak or would be seen "as a doormat." In fact, forgiveness needed courage and integrity. It also didn't mean that he was condoning what other people had done wrong, or that he should expect to be reconciled with the people who had upset him.

Gary came to realize that carrying around feelings of anger and resentment was not good for his mental or physical health. Far from it: he was also carrying a heavy burden of stress. Practicing empathy and letting a little compassion flow would be healing. In fact, forgiveness was in his own best interest. He needed it for himself.

As a starter exercise, Gary was advised to put himself in the shoes of the people who he felt had hurt him, and try to empathize with them. The group reminded him that most of us have been in situations where we betrayed or hurt others. Nobody is perfect. Instead of nursing feelings of revenge, resentment, and judgment, it would be much more productive to be generous, compassionate, and kind. One of the participants told Gary the story of two political prisoners who met after many years, having been released from captivity. The first man asked, "Have you forgiven your jailers?" The second man replied, "No, and I will never be able to." "Then," said the first ex-prisoner, "I guess you're still in prison."

Like the second prisoner, practicing forgiving didn't come easily to Gary. He went through periods of grief, rage, sorrow, fear, and confusion. But as time passed, he understood that forgiveness really was a gift to himself—a way to end his negative outlook on life. It was a way to find greater peace and provide closure. He gave up expecting things from other people that they would never be able to give. He began to turn his energy in more positive directions. Taking these steps gave him greater freedom and greater peace of mind.

The power of forgiveness can heal in a way no medication or treatment can. A life well lived may be the best revenge for wounded feelings. Gary learned that by putting more energy into appreciating what he had rather than obsessing about what he didn't have was a much more constructive way of dealing with life.

Questions

- What does the word "forgiveness" mean to you?
- How do you react when people hurt you?
- Do you find it easy to forgive? And what do you do to be able to forgive?
- If you find forgiveness very difficult, what do you think prevents you from getting there? Why do you find it so hard?
- Do you think you should continue to have a forgiving attitude if someone continues to hurt you?
- What do you think will happen to you if you don't forgive?
- How will you know if you have forgiven someone? What are the indicators? Do you have any idea how to deal with residual anger and resentment?

14

Thank You Kindly

On Gratitude

The corporate culture at Nexobank was toxic. Some even described the working environment as "Darwinian"—it was survival of the fittest. Everyone seemed to be out for themselves and teamwork was nonexistent. What's more, greed, bullying, and even plain illegal behavior were rampant. Singularly focused on profits and bonuses, the senior leadership team whittled away at their employees' self-confidence, health, and sanity. The results were decreased productivity, low morale, serious absenteeism, and a disturbingly high employee turnover. For many, working at the bank had become an emotionally draining experience.

Senior management perpetuated the cold, calculating, and impersonal culture. They didn't seem to realize the importance of creating a work environment where people could be friendly, cooperative, and supportive. It never dawned on them that a culture of positive regard and genuine caring would foster creativity and new ideas, that gratitude for work well done could be a great motivating force. Instead, most employees felt undervalued and taken for granted. And given the bank's toxic culture, it was no surprise when a number of its traders were implicated in the Libor scandal of fixing interest rates. The legal actions that followed led to serious fines, although none of the top executives seemed to have been affected.

M.F.R. Kets de Vries, *Riding the Leadership Rollercoaster*,
DOI 10.1007/978-3-319-45162-6_14

As this example illustrates, a toxic culture—an environment where the word "gratitude" does not exist—can spiral into actions that lead to business failure. When money is viewed as the singular motivator, those in charge of the organization will not be able to engage hearts and minds and get the best out of their people. This is because what really counts for most people, apart from receiving a fair wage, are respect, recognition, and a sense of accomplishment, belonging, and purpose.

To foster a corporate culture that includes these variables, leaders need to create a place of work where gratitude takes pride of place. When people are exposed to everyday acts of kindness, a simple "thank you" for work well done can be a great motivator and contribute to a more positive work environment.

The words grateful and gratitude have their origins in the Latin "*gratus*," meaning the readiness to show appreciation for kindness and return it. Grateful people count their blessings, have the ability to appreciate the simple pleasures of life, and are always prepared to acknowledge the good things that happen to them. They are also the kinds of people who are willing to give something back.

Philosophers throughout the ages have seen gratitude as an important contributor to harmonious relationships. As the philosopher-emperor Marcus Aurelius noted: "Take full account of the excellencies which you possess, and in gratitude remember how you would hanker after them, if you had them not." Psychoanalysts, too, have shown considerable interest in the subject, viewing gratitude as the more mature antithesis to the early envy that characterizes infant behavior. As gratitude develops, so does our capacity for expressing appreciation in our future relationships. Gratitude is the glue that builds reciprocity.

As a matter of fact, the relationship between gratitude and pro-social behavior is very complex. The quality of the connections we make with our caregivers affects the way our infant brain develops. When a secure attachment is established in our early years, a sound foundation is put into place that will color the way we deal with others throughout our life. It will determine our resilience when coping with stress, our effectiveness in balancing our emotions; how secure we will be in exploring the world;

and how hopefully we will look to the future. Securely attached people find it easier to express and receive gratitude. In contrast, attachment insecurity affects social behavior negatively. Insecure people find it harder to be at the receiving end of gratitude, or to express it. They seem to lack the developmental resources—like empathy and compassion—to do so.

Much about gratitude also has to do with the perspective we take, the framework we use to look at the world and at ourselves. Grateful people build optimism into their everyday lives. They know how to redraw their unconscious frames of comparison in a positive and valuable light. They are more likely to let go of their past, accept the present, and look forward to the future. Grateful people focus on what they have instead of lamenting what they lack.

Research has shown that the capacity to express gratitude improves both physical and mental health. Practicing gratitude releases the positive mood-enhancing neurotransmitter serotonin in our brain. Taking a grateful stance when faced with difficulties and setbacks—consciously looking for a silver lining or working at positive reframing—converts negative stress into positive energy. It can provide the momentum needed to overcome life's challenges. We might even say that gratitude is a natural form of anti-depressant.

This all sounds wonderful in theory but how can we practice gratitude? How can we create environments where people are recognized for their work and in return will strive to give their best? How do we avoid finding ourselves in toxic organizations like Nexobank?

The first and most basic thing is to respect the people who work in the organization. Just as gratitude evokes cooperative responses, it also creates mutually supportive relationships, helps neutralize conflict, generates positive energy, and fosters a collective "we're all in this together" mentality. Gratitude in practice also means giving people due recognition, fair treatment, creating a sense of belonging, and providing them with voice. If senior management recognizes these important dynamics, the results in terms of improving the wellness factor in the organization, increasing employee satisfaction and creating better results at work can be astonishing.

A concrete action is to make a daily habit of deciding, on waking or getting up in the morning, what our outlook is going to be. Are we going to be consciously grateful for what we have, or are we going to be negative and moan? This might be difficult at times (we all have our bad days); however, we need to learn to stop whining. Complaining does very little but produce ineffectual hot air but the outlook we decide to adopt and our subsequent actions can make a difference.

Another action is to devote some time each day to reflecting on the various things we should be grateful for. Like many clichés, the old imperative to "count your blessings" is repeated for a reason. Making this a purposeful exercise can be illuminating. We should enumerate the people we should be grateful to who influence our lives in a positive way and thank them for it. We should also try to surround ourselves with people who practice gratitude themselves.

Of course, it isn't realistic to suggest that we should never express negativity or doubt. We need to address the negative aspects of our life as well as the positive. However, it is better for our mental health to make an effort to calibrate our outlook towards the positive. Even life's greatest challenges can be reframed as opportunities for significant personal growth and development. Conversely, ruminating on negative thoughts drains us of energy and motivation. When we turn our narcissistic gaze away from ourselves toward others, we often feel much better.

I like to think that in dealing with life's vicissitudes we are like painters. We have to decide what colors to paint our life in, murky or bright? And like painters, we have to think about composition: what are we going to put in the foreground? How are we going to make all the components work together? Humor, forgiveness, and gratitude are the brightest colors in the palette. If we use them in our life's journey, we will be painting ourselves a more positive, fulfilling, and vibrant life.

Questions

- What are you grateful for? And are you clear what you should be grateful for? Are there things you take for granted but shouldn't?
- What did you do today that you enjoyed? What made you feel good?

- Can you list the people in your life who have been helpful to you? What kinds of relationships are you grateful for?
- Have you ever expressed your gratitude to these people? Have you ever told them what they mean to you?
- Are there people who have expressed gratitude to you?
- Do you know ways to say "thank you" more often? Are there ways you can be more helpful to others?

15

Every Seven Seconds
Sexuality in the Workplace

This is what a senior executive once told me about sex:

> Whenever I have to deal with sexual desire, it's a tragedy-in-the-making. Frankly, there have been quite a few times when I lost control. All the mistakes I made in my life have been because of sex. I have been married several times. Two of my wives I met at work. In both cases we were working together on a project. At the time, when I got involved, I knew I was playing with fire. I'm the guy Robin Williams made that joke about—you know—God gave us a penis and a brain, but only enough blood to run one at a time. That's me.

I have had this conversation many times, with many men who have had difficulty dealing with the sexual cloud that hovers over the workplace.

A large body of research has shown that men think about sex much more often than women do—the myth is every seven seconds, when awake, and even asleep men are far more likely than women to dream of sexual encounters. So how easy is it for a man to be just a friend or work "colleague" with a woman he finds attractive? It's a point famously debated in the film *When Harry Met Sally*. Harry maintains it's impos-

M.F.R. Kets de Vries, *Riding the Leadership Rollercoaster*,
DOI 10.1007/978-3-319-45162-6_15

sible for a man to be friends with a woman he finds attractive because he always wants to have sex with her. When Sally asks whether a man can be friends with a woman he finds unattractive, Harry replies, "No, you pretty much want to nail 'em too." Given the frequency and intensity of male fantasies, are platonic relationships with the female sex possible? And how does the sexual dimension affect male–female relationships in a business setting? What role does the sexual cloud play in the delicate issue of the lack of women in the C-suite?

One of the key explanations for the underrepresentation of women at the top levels of organizations or on boards is the lack of fit between women's "natural" strengths and the qualities needed for leadership. Women are stereotyped as being more "communal," and associated with qualities like friendliness, selflessness, and emotional expressiveness. In contrast, men are viewed as more "agentic," with qualities that are more congruent with the image of an effective executive, like independence, assertiveness, and competence. Moreover, women are caught in a double bind. The more directive a woman's behavior, the less favorably both men and women will perceive her. Instead of being admired for her boldness and initiative, she is typecast as pushy, bossy, and uncaring. As the movie star Bette Davis once said, "When a man gives his opinion, he's a man. When a woman gives her opinion, she's a bitch."

Despite social and economical advancement, people today are still governed by same sexual desires that drove our primitive ancestors. Approximately 200,000 years of genetic legacy cannot be brushed away by sophisticated social attitudes to gender equality. At an unconscious, biological level, men are still driven to maximize their genetic legacy. But women's relationship with sex, the legacy of the same evolutionary process, is very different. Women exercise much more discretion to ensure the commitment of their partner's economic, emotional, and sexual resources. Unlike men, who produce millions of new sperm daily throughout most of their lifetime, women are born with up to two million immature eggs of which only about 400 ever mature. Given the limited supply of eggs, our female ancestors always had to be extremely careful in selecting their mates, which made for a very different orientation with respect to male–female interactions.

I suggest that this primal sexual desire in men and anxiety about the consequences of sexual attraction (especially in a professional context) is a contributing factor to the reluctance of men to allow women entry into the upper echelons of an organization. It requires a tremendous effort to deflect men's attention from their sexual feelings, a "management process" made even more challenging by many men's false assumption that women think like them, a perception which can make for a very volatile cocktail. This may be one explanation of the frequency of women's complaints of sexual harassment in the workplace. It has been estimated that more than one out of three women have been exposed to some form of unwanted sexual attention in their lifetime.

From a psychodynamic point of view, men's ambivalence about the seductive powers of women is a red thread running throughout human history, symbolized by a very archaic, masculine fear of women in general. These concerns manifest themselves in many different cultural contexts, with the universal storyline that too many seductive women lure men into destruction. Women, as seductresses, are held responsible for the downfall of their men. For example, in the Hindu religion, the goddess Kali is associated not only with motherly love, but also with death, sexuality, and violence. As the goddess of destruction, she destroys only to recreate. In Buddhism, Mara is the demon who tried to destroy Gautama Buddha's quest for enlightenment by attempting to seduce him with a vision of beautiful women. In the Judeo-Christian tradition, stories of devouring, castrating, even spider-like women are ubiquitous. In Islamic culture, there is an implicit and explicit fear of the seductive, sexual power of women, explaining the need for their seclusion and surveillance. In contemporary popular culture, films like *Basic Instinct*, in which a woman kills a man with an ice pick after sex, reveal that this theme is still as lively and recognizable today. So, given that looming sexual cloud, why not play safe and take preventive action? Keep women out—working too closely with them may disrupt organizational processes and lead to trouble.

One of the factors on which a country's economic progress depends is human capital. If we don't provide women with adequate access to employment opportunities, we will lose at least half our potential. Gender inequality is not just a women's issue. It affects us all. The exclusion of women's potential lowers the quality of life for both men and women in organizations. While women bear the largest and most direct costs of these inequalities, these costs cut broadly across society, ultimately hindering social and economic development. If senior executives are really serious about fair process in organizations, they need to be upfront about understanding how the sexual dimension affects organizational dynamics. Men and women should resist becoming the pawns of evolutionary drivers. Sexism is a social and therefore curable disease. Given the possibility of choice, what can be done to create organizations in which both men and women can thrive? I suggest three main approaches to answering this question.

The first is raising awareness. This is the first step toward tackling the problem of subtle gender discrimination. Senior executives need to acknowledge that most organizations are not women-friendly and recognize that men and women have different needs, including career-specific needs. It is self-evident that the creation of more women-friendly organizations starts at the top, with the willingness to experiment with other forms of organizational identities and create a more inclusive culture. To enable change, both men and women need to become more consciously aware of their biases and how implicit gender norms (consciously or unconsciously) are keeping women out. Part of the awareness-raising program should be paying attention to how the sexual cloud interferes with reasoning and behavior.

The second approach is systemic, structural intervention. If awareness is a start, the next step is the institutionalization of structural measures. The structure of most contemporary organizations is still very hierarchical, characterized by top-down leadership, individual achievement, and task orientation. Where women are in leadership positions, we see more network-oriented structures, a greater emphasis on team effort, and a greater preference for people-oriented skills such as teaching, mentoring, and coaching. In general, more female-oriented organizations are also characterized by flatter, more flexible organizational structures where power, authority, and decision-making are more decentralized.

To make organizations more gender neutral, more creative performance indicators, compensation and benefits systems, and career track systems need to be put in place. In particular, this implies paying respect (and not just lip service) to the work–life balance by providing flexitime, alternative schedules, part-time and home working, compressed working weeks, and job sharing. Much of this boils down to finding ways to create effective support systems when children enter the equation. Organizations also need to adapt to the different commitment intensities of the different phases of the executive career cycle.

Top management also needs to nurture an inclusive, supportive, and respectful cultural environment in which inappropriate sexual innuendo and sexualized behavior have no part. Organizational culture needs to adapt to the qualities and needs of all its constituents, and continuously evolve to allow both men and women to flourish equally.

The third approach is gender-equal development. From a developmental point of view, practices like awareness raising and intervention are delayed, stopgap measures. The real starting point for any change needs to take place much earlier when gender roles are established and reinforced with early child-rearing practices. Gender dynamics start with the role models provided by parents and the way certain activities and abilities are characterized as masculine or feminine, agentic or communal. We should aim to bring up children without gender discrimination so that they are free to have the feminine and masculine attributes that fit them best. Children who develop more flexible, androgynous gender identities will be better prepared to cope with the stresses of life in contemporary society.

Only when our social expectations for men and women are equal will we surpass our social prejudices and their limitations, so that women can take up their places in the C-suite. Senior executives who really care about fair process in organizations have the obligation to manage the sexual cloud more effectively. They need to engage in more systemic measures to counteract deeply embedded assumptions about gender and role expectations and to create more inclusive organizations in which both men and women will thrive.

Questions

- How does your organization treat women? Have you experienced gender discrimination? In meetings you attend, are women routinely asked to make notes, sort out refreshments, or plan parties?
- Are there many women in your talent pipeline? What percentage of them are in senior executive positions?
- Are pay and benefits the same for men and women in your organization?
- As a woman, have you been exposed to intimate and inappropriate questions and behavior? For example, have you been asked, "Do you want children?" "Why don't you want kids?" or "How can you leave your kids?" Have you even been exposed to unwanted sexual advances?
- What is your organization doing to make life easier for couples with children? How does it accommodate women in terms of pregnancy and maternity leave?
- As a parent, do you treat girls and boys differently? Do you avoid using stereotypes in career discussions?

16

Just Get on With It

Getting Things Done

Top executives need to realize that execution of strategy is not an abstract exercise. It involves people. And getting people to work together toward a common goal is not a given. As many senior executives have learned the hard way, getting everyone on the same page can be an uphill struggle. Even if people have the will to follow a certain path, they may not have the skills to get them there. They may engage in the kind of behavior that makes teamwork very difficult.

By the age of 30, our personality tends to be relatively stable but this does not mean that we are incapable of changing the way we behave and act at later stages in our life. However, later behavior change is not easy. Many senior executives are at the summit of their career trajectory, and have got there as a result of habitual behavior patterns. Although it may be apparent to others that aspects of an executive's behavior are dysfunctional, the individual in question may see no compelling reason to change behavior patterns that have yielded results thus far. As a result, many cling to habitual behavior hoping for a different outcome and if this doesn't happen, put the blame on others. Even if these executives are willing to make an effort to change, they don't really know how to do things differently.

M.F.R. Kets de Vries, *Riding the Leadership Rollercoaster*,
DOI 10.1007/978-3-319-45162-6_16

Busy executives who want to reinvent themselves to become more effective leaders, often look for expedient quick fixes. Clearly, the challenge is to develop a method of intervention that is similar to more traditional therapeutic approaches but in a way that is perceived as effective and manageable for executives. This is where the group coaching methodology can play an important role. Let me give an example.

Pushed to action by rapid evolution in the petroleum industry, the executive team of a global energy company knew they had to transform their solid but complacent organization into a hi-tech, sustainability-oriented firm. To facilitate this transition, the CEO had hired Jim, a brilliant professor of engineering, as the new Chief Knowledge Officer. Around the same time, another executive was asked to join the team as VP Technology, Products, and Services. John was an experienced executive in the petroleum industry who was seconded by one of the major shareholders to put into operation a large offshore drilling project. However, these two new additions worsened what was already a rather ineffective decision-making body. True to form, within several months of Jim and John's arrival, war had broken out between these outsiders and the other members of the executive team.

The company was heavily committed to its offshore energy project, making it necessary to meet specific deadlines—and pressures were mounting. Although overruns would be extremely costly, there seemed to be a lack of urgency among the members of the executive team to move the project forward. Instead, turf wars for resources seemed to be more important than goal alignment and working for the common good. All of the executive team members, without exception, were failing in the execution of its intended goals. The absence of clear objectives and agreed processes resulted in unsuccessful execution of the organization's strategy.

The CEO decided to bring everyone on the senior executive team together for what he called a high-performance team intervention. The objective would be to reflect on their interpersonal relationships, work practices, leadership styles, and the organizational culture, guided by an experienced group coach. The underlying agenda, however, was to create alignment and become more effective in implementing the corporate transformation process.

It didn't take much effort for me, as group coach, to find out that company morale was low, the transformation process was stalled, the offshore project was facing expensive delays, and they were on a fast track into the red. The executive committee was not really a team but a group of ships passing in the night, each with a different destination. They were unable to drive a consistent action plan deep down into the organization and to unify and fully engage their employees toward the execution of its organizational objectives.

I began the team intervention with a short lecture about high-performance organizations and effective leadership. Then to break the ice and instill a more playful mood, I asked each member of the executive committee to draw a self-portrait, a picture of what was in their head, heart, stomach, past, present, work, and leisure. After initial grumbling and skepticism, all the executives became immersed in this task. When the self-portraits were completed and displayed on the wall, I asked Jim if he would like to kick off the process by telling the group about his drawing.

We learned that Jim's grandfather had been a brilliant academic but his father's life was marked by failure rather than success and the disappointment of one lost job after another. Jim had spent a great deal of time with his grandfather, who found in him the enthusiasm and curiosity that his own son seemed to lack. As a result Jim's identity as a researcher had become very important to him. In his present role with the company, he felt his creativity might be stifled, so he did whatever he could to protect what he called the "spark," keeping his fellow executive team members at a distance. Being too much of a team member carried the concern of being just average. Also, he had an underlying fear that he would become like his father and waste away his talents.

Now, looking at the information from the 360° feedback reports, and listening to the challenging but supportive comments from the group, he realized that other people found this behavior obstructive, aggravating existing problems with the team and the company.

Each member of the executive team, including the CEO, went through the same process. Each took the "hot seat" to tell his or her story and was given constructive feedback by the group, in the process discovering surprising things about each other. The exercise forced all the executives to face the fact that their current actions reinforced the company's prevalent silo behavior, didn't facilitate organizational learning, prevented alignment, and hampered execution. Having accepted this, they were able to think constructively and with the support of the other members of the group to think about how they could modify or accommodate the problematic behaviors. Jim, for example, promised to be present at meetings where his expertise was really needed, and to be more responsive to email. He also decided to hire an assistant who would help him be better organized. The members of the team, on their part, agreed not to harass him with minor issues, and respect his need for reflection time.

Each of the participants listed specific behavior changes they would focus on to facilitate communication and collaboration with the other team members. The intervention was concluded with an action plan for each of them to identify ways in which they could all contribute to the team's alignment and become better at execution. The session included recommendations at the end to ensure clear process and accountability.

Through the group coaching process, all the executives gained considerable insights into their own and others' strengths and weaknesses. They recognized the complementarity of their skills—how together they could have much more impact. They promised to coach each other whenever one of them strayed from his or her specific action points. For the first time, they had their first real team debate to obtain clarity about the direction the company had to take and committed themselves to actions that would make them better at execution.

At a follow-up meeting several months later, I learned that the members of the executive team now felt they had become more effective as a group. There was a greater openness among them, real dialogue, greater exchange of ideas, more accountability, more trust, and less management by fear. Decisions were being implemented and the company was seeing progress and moving forward. Many of the executives expressed their astonishment at the extent to which they had bonded after such a short workshop.

The group coaching intervention had proved to be a great way to create a truly networked organization, as it minimized the paranoid thinking that had previously been the norm within the company's virtual, highly diverse teams. It had broken down the silo mentality and opened up the path toward becoming a more boundaryless organization engaged in real information exchange. Now, all members of the executive team were prepared to contribute to a more agile, learning organization. Last, but not least, the group coaching experience had helped them to be more effective in dealing with the major weakness that had hindered their organization for so long: execution.

Questions

- Would you like to have a more network-oriented organization but as things stand, does your organization seem to be far from that goal?
- Given the way the top team interacts, is it difficult to reach an overarching, unified vision?
- Are you a learning organization? Do different parts of your organization learn from each other? Or do you think that your organization is too silo driven? Is information sharing among the various constituencies in your organization difficult? To what extent is silo behavior linked to the incentive system?
- Do you find your meetings seem endless, boring—not going anywhere? Is there a lack of prioritization?
- If your meetings are ineffective, is this because overt and covert conflict between participants is not addressed? Could it have something to do with a lack of trust and mutual respect among executives?
- During these meetings, are decisions taken that are never implemented? Is execution a problem in your organization? Do you think that some members of your organization are engaged in subtle sabotage—passive-aggressive behavior?

17

"Yo Suis ein European"

Identity Issues

Look up Europe on the Internet and the top site tells you that Europe is "a continent that comprises the westernmost part of Eurasia." Yet how many people who grew up, live, work, or simply visit Europe today really think of its geography or its national boundaries? How do people born in one of the European Union's member states define what it means to be European? Here's Carlos's answer to that question:

> You ask me about my national identity, and I have a difficult time responding. My mother is Spanish. My father is German. My wife is Swedish. Sweden is the country where I grew up. Now I'm living in the UK. I'm also supposed to be a European. To make things more complicated, there are several religions in my close family. We have Roman Catholics, Lutherans, Muslims, Jews, and even Buddhists. When people ask where I come from, I find it difficult to give an answer that feels right. I remember struggling with this confusion very early in my life. It created problems for me at school. All through my life I've had episodes of disconnectedness, feeling rootless, with no sense of purpose. Even now, I don't really know who I am. I know I should be flourishing with the cultural richness of my background but instead I often feel empty. What's going on?

M.F.R. Kets de Vries, *Riding the Leadership Rollercoaster*,
DOI 10.1007/978-3-319-45162-6_17

Carlos is in the middle of a national identity crisis and one of the reasons may be his multinational European roots. Unable to identify with a specific nation, region, or language, he is struggling with what he perceives as a nebulous European identity. His confusion brings us to a very basic question: what is identity? The term can be very puzzling. It exists on multiple levels: cultural, gender, professional role, position in the family, religious affiliation, and so on. But however we define identity, it takes shape through social action. As a construct, identity is based on differences (what I am not) and belonging (what I am). Through difference or belonging, we position who we are. This means that we rarely have only one identity; in fact, we may have many and they may exist in varying degrees of tension with one another, as Carlos's story illustrates. Our identity changes over time and is captured and reinforced in the stories people tell about themselves to give continuity to their experience. Carlos, a German-Spanish Swedish-born European, struggles to tell a consistent narrative.

He may also be a "victim" of the European experiment. The nation states of Europe have become less clearly defined. Identities are now diluted and no longer consist of discrete wholes anchored in somewhat unique cultures and territorial nation-states. Although the opening up of cultures to one another is supposed to be an enriching experience, it can also result in great confusion. It also contributes to paranoid reactions, feelings that are easily exploited by demagogues.

Fortunately, not everyone is subject to this crisis of identity. Those who have a strong sense of inner security can use this multicultural heritage to their advantage. Identifying as a European can make them more effective in a global environment, and better world citizens, fulfilling what the founding fathers of the European Economic Community originally had in mind. The founding fathers of Europe were preoccupied by the pacification of Europe, not via a balance of power, but via the reconciliation of European nations—and the prevention of future wars. All of them signed up to the idea of European unity.

However, only a small percentage of people in Europe will say that they feel first and foremost "European." The greatest challenge to a single European identity is the fact that Europe is multilingual. There is no common language that can be used with equal ease by its different constituents. Any attempt to introduce English, the most common second language in most countries, as the lingua franca has been met with great resistance, reflecting national sensitivities and pride. There are also significant religious differences within Europe, which has had a strong influence on legal matters, in particular marriage law. These religious differences, in turn, affect values, beliefs, attitudes, and behavior, and unavoidably impact on the way people work and relate to one another.

When people feel insecure about their identity, like Carlos, xenophobic feelings start to emerge. Xenophobia is rooted in the fear of losing one's own culture and identity to another—in this case Europe and beyond. It is especially expressed toward immigrants outside their national and European borders. But despite such regressive, even paranoid behavior, the social, political, cultural, and geographical perceptions that Europeans have of each other have changed dramatically over the last five decades. Within the territory covered by the Schengen Treaty, national borders, although still very relevant to many people's collective identity, are no longer obstacles to mobility for the large majority of Europe's population. The present-day European Union is now the single most important institutional structure in Europe. The euro currency, notwithstanding its difficulties, is in many ways another major milestone in the process of the "Europeanization of Europe."

The shared heritage of the people of Europe has contributed to a number of very distinguished features. For example, one of the characteristics of being a European is to value the social responsibility of the state, which most Europeans also associate with a social safety net. Of course, there are variations among the EU nations in the extent to which their populations rely on the government in their daily lives. There are welfare states where citizens can expect to benefit from the redistribution of wealth, and countries where they are expected to be more self-reliant. But whatever the case may be, quality of life ranks high on their list of priorities, as do environmental concerns. Also, Europeans value education as a human right and the government is expected to play an important role in this. Maintaining peace is a critical issue. The EU nations are now very reluctant to use military means to achieve political goals. Europeans value citizens' rights to protest, dissent, achieve justice, and live without fear, censorship, poverty, hatred, and prejudice. They support gender equality and respect for other ethnic groups. They believe that democracy is the least bad form of government. With the recent expansion to the east, some members of the EU have lived under communism. They know its negative implications, and carry these experiences into their new European organizational life.

Another distinguishing feature of the European identity is investment in shared cultural experiences, such as a European movie and music industry, other forms of art, education, as well as constant exchanges of culture experiences. Education, especially, both in the formal academic sense, and informally through the media, has also been a primary tool in bolstering a European identity. Given the different educational systems within European countries (with often incompatible curricula and requirements), however, there has been a strong trend toward the unification of degree-granting rules and procedures, so that levels of educational attainment will be similar. The Erasmus university exchange program of young Europeans to study and work across the continent can also be seen as a unifying force.

Another movement toward the direction of unification has been the massive convergence of patterns of consumption and lifestyles. But still, in spite of these various forces for harmonization, two opposing consumer trends continue to coexist, one that emphasizes the importance of national identity and the right to difference, and the other that advocates the right for a common identity.

These developmental streams have contributed to an evolving model of European leadership, quite distinct from the American one—a unique model that can be highly effective in our global world. Some of these distinct European patterns also contribute to a more sustainable, long-term focused form of leadership. For example, while the American style of leadership includes a bias toward short-term gains, an inordinate focus on capital markets and finance, and an over-simplistic understanding of the concept of shareholder value, Europe's leadership orientation can be described as a more responsible kind of capitalism held in check by the institutions of civil society. The European leadership model is more rooted in a long-term mentality. Granted, the European consensus-orientated leadership style comes at the price of speed. But although pace and execution can be slower under the European model, once everyone is involved and on board in the decision-making process, the execution of decisions becomes increasingly rapid.

In Europe, change tends to occur incrementally rather than by rupture or breakthrough. We can hypothesize one outcome of this, in that Americans develop more innovative management techniques and styles, and may be quicker to adapt them. Europeans, in contrast, may be slower to adopt but more thorough in implementation. Given their more social outlook, Europeans tend to be less market-economy driven, less competitive. They tend to have a stronger belief in societal values, a greater concern for quality of life, and a greater preoccupation about people's well-being, which creates a different outlook toward motivation and how to treat people at work.

Being cognizant of what it means to be a European (and in spite of his perceived identity crisis), Carlos should be aware that having such a rich heritage is a great blessing, especially in a world that has become truly international, and where organizations themselves have also become increasingly global. He should realize that a national *and* a European identity could co-exist provided that he believes that he can benefit both individually and as a member of different identities from such arrangements. But as his confusion indicates, the making of a European identity can also produce uncertainty and vulnerability among some, depriving them of a stable point of reference. Carlos's confusion could be alleviated, however, by changing his orientation, accepting the contradictions, acknowledging that his identity is a work in progress, working toward becoming a true European.

Questions

- Have you reflected on what it means to be a European? Do you like being part of Europe, or do you have mixed feelings?
- Do you have an idea how both individual and national identities are formed, as well as how these identities influence your outlook, your behavior, and your way of making decisions?

- Are you preoccupied with questions of national identity? If so, are you clear about your country's social values and norms—your shared culture?
- Do you have any idea how you can be *you* in today's world—how you will be able to adapt to the changes taking place and yet retain a sense of cultural continuity?
- Have you experienced any change in the way you view your national identity over time? Do you think you are moving away from your parents' values?
- Do you think it is possible to adapt to the changes taking place around you without losing touch with the past? Do you have any idea how you can reconcile this dilemma? Do you sometimes feel "stuck in the middle"?
- Do you feel threatened by the migration of people from other countries into your country? If so, how do you respond to this?

18

If You Can Make It There …

Global Coaching

The move to Brazil was turning out to be more complex than Augusto had expected. The whole experience had been a real culture shock. The family was having a hard time adapting to their new life, and it hadn't been easy for the children to start a new school. Although they had overcome the language barrier very quickly, they missed their friends back home. Augusto and Marion had presented the move as an adventure but the reality turned out to be quite different. To start with, there were the hassles with the house. Workmen promised to come but rarely kept their promises. They seemed not to have heard of schedules—unlike Marion. They had relocated to São Paulo following her appointment as head of sales for Latin America. Now Marion, worried about her new responsibilities and feeling abandoned by her home office, spent long hours at work, came home exhausted, made a half-hearted effort to read a story to the children, and was then absorbed by her email before collapsing into bed. They hardly seemed to speak any more and their sex life was non-existent. When Augusto complained about the way the marriage was going, Marion would retort that he was drinking too much. But what was so wrong with having a few drinks to relax?

M.F.R. Kets de Vries, *Riding the Leadership Rollercoaster,*
DOI 10.1007/978-3-319-45162-6_18

As an academic, Augusto had hoped to find a professorship at a Brazilian university but that, too, was not the shoo-in he'd imagined. Perhaps this was not such a bad thing after all: he would have the time and inspiration to work on his novel. But his writing was going nowhere; there were just too many things to be taken care of.

Augusto fantasized increasingly about returning home. The only positive thing to have happened recently was that Marion, who had seemed to ignore the way he was feeling, was showing signs of concern. Perhaps it was dawning on her that if things continued as they were, they could end up going their separate ways.

Of course, Marion had been aware of her husband's unhappiness but the demands of her new job and the fact that she was the only breadwinner, were her overwhelming preoccupations. The turning point came when she had lunch with an old friend who was visiting São Paulo. An executive coach and psychotherapist, he was a good listener. Even better, having heard her worries, he put her in touch with an executive coach in the city—someone very experienced in dealing with expatriates.

This turned out to be a very positive experience. The coach proposed working with Marion and Augusto to help them work through their marital difficulties. In the process, she provided them with many insights about the way of living in Brazil—how decisions were made and how work would get done. In particular, she helped Augusto cope better with his new role, his environment and local culture, making him feel less disconnected. Her interventions with Marion helped her to get greater clarity about the career implications of taking a position abroad. She explored with her what to do to be better supported by the home office. In fact, the coach's inputs were invaluable in helping the couple to deal with adjustment problems.

Why, Augusto wondered, had Marion's company not been more proactive when they moved her to Brazil? The coach had made it clear that their difficulties were by no means unusual. Why had there never been any briefing about how to deal with cultural differences? He felt they had both been set up for failure rather than success. The company didn't seem to have anything close to a culturally appropriate corporate plan. Head office had left Marion high and dry: there was no clarity about how her time in Brazil would support her longer-term career, nor any indication of the assistance they could expect when she was eventually repatriated.

Stories such as Marion and Augusto's lie behind the failure of a significant number of expatriate assignments. As their coach told them, theirs was the typical scenario: an executive is reassigned to a foreign country and engrossed in the new job, while the spouse is left to deal with all the hassles of settling in. If the transition to a new culture isn't done well, expatriate assignments can make or break a relationship or marriage. The situation is often aggravated when spouses cannot pursue their own career in the new country, or even experience restrictions to their personal freedom. Some kind of identity crisis, due to the loss of independence and status, is a frequent occurrence. The match between lifecycle and career cycle also plays a critical role in the success or failure of assignments, as executives are more mobile at some stages in life than others.

The rate of failure of expatriate assignments fluctuates between 10% and 50%, depending on the country in question. Being transferred to an emerging economy has a higher chance for failure than being sent to a developed one. The inability to adapt to the new culture, to cope with the challenges associated with an expatriate assignment, and having to deal with limited spousal employment opportunities have all been cited as significant factors in failed expatriate assignments. Cross-cultural coaching, specifically for couples and their families, can limit the possibility of failure but unfortunately there are not many companies that assess marital and family motivation and psychological preparedness for accepting an expatriate assignment. The non-availability of such services is puzzling, not only because of the cost of expatriating executives, but also because the success of an assignment is heavily dependent on the expatriate's spouse and wider family.

For too many companies, the primary criterion for choosing an executive to work abroad is technical competence. If executives have done a good job at home, the assumption is that they will do an equally stellar job in another country. Preparing them for working in a different culture or context does not seem to come into it. After all, executives are supposed to be able to sort out the problems that come their way—if something goes wrong, they should be able to fix it.

Technical skills are undeniably necessary for certain assignments—overseeing the set-up of a new plant, the expansion of a factory, or the establishment of a new office—but they are not sufficient. Certain interpersonal qualities and attitudes are also needed to make an assignment a success or a failure, particularly at higher-level executive positions.

A major factor making assignments successful is cultural adaptability. The most commonly listed variables that determine cultural adaptability are open-mindedness, self-confidence, ability to deal with ambiguity, ability to relate to people (being collaborative), and curiosity. Other factors include mental flexibility, a stable marriage or relationship, having had previous social and cross-cultural exposure, and physical and emotional stamina, all weighted according to country and type of job. Culturally adaptable executives find it easier to move from one culture to another.

I have learned from experience that the greater the consideration paid during the selection process to a candidate's emotional intelligence, the higher the success rate of the assignment. Unfortunately, criteria for selection are all too frequently developed in a vacuum. The advice of host-country nationals—the people who are actually going to work with the expatriate manager—is rarely sought at the selection stage.

Another extremely important element of an expatriate's success or failure is the experience of spouse and children. The most frequent reason for an executive's failing to complete an assignment in another country is the negative reaction of the spouse. Despite this, very few companies interview spouses during the selection procedure, and a still smaller percentage include spouses in training programs. The failure to recognize this can be a costly omission for both the company and the family.

Upbringing and personality also play a role in the success or failure of assignments. For example, the more intercultural experiences children have early in life, the more likely they are to develop the kind of cultural empathy necessary for leadership effectiveness as adults when working for a global company. Exposure in childhood to different nationalities and languages can be a determining factor in how well an adult deals with cultural diversity later in life. Children of mixed-culture marriages, bilingual parents, diplomats, or executives who move frequently have the advantage of exposure to diverse cultural contexts.

In psychological terms, I have noted that successful expatriates have slightly paradoxical characteristics. On the one hand, they need to be chameleons—that is, they need to have the flexibility to pick up signals from their environment and to mold themselves and their behavior to blend in. The downside of such high adaptability is that it may be interpreted as being emotionally and socially shallow. On the other hand, they also need a set of resilient core values that guide and support them in whatever environment they find themselves. The challenge is to combine their resilience and their plasticity. This does not necessarily have to be a contradiction. "Going native" is not the answer, but neither is staying aloof from the host culture. A middle ground must be found.

For companies that proactively prepare their executives for international assignments, international executive development courses are fast becoming a requirement for grooming future global leaders. Many organizations send promising young executives to international executive programs outside their home country—fertile ground for developing cultural awareness and adaptability. Many of the activities in these programs are done in multinational study groups. Participants must work closely together on a variety of projects; to succeed, they must develop a cross-cultural mindset. This process effectively minimizes ethnocentricity.

On-the-job training offers education of another sort, and is no less vital. Exposure to international leadership experiences—P&L responsibility—early in a career is important. These experiences should include working in multicultural teams. This kind of early international experience is a good test of a young executive's global leadership potential because they hone the capacity to cope with the difficult leadership challenges they will meet later on.

Global companies need to ensure that cross-cultural coaching is available in every international executive development program and throughout the duration of an expatriate assignment. Enlisting the help of executive coaches with experience of working in an international context can support expatriates and their families dealing with the many challenges that emerge during the course of an expatriate assignment. Making this part of an expatriation package will be a win–win proposition for all the parties involved.

Questions

- What advice would you give a person leaving on a foreign assignment?
- If you were asked to take on an expatriate assignment, are there people in your organization who you could turn to, who could explain the culture of the country to which you are going, and know people who could be part of your network?
- Does your organization provide cross-cultural training? Does it pay attention to the adaptability of your spouse and children?
- What about repatriation? Has your organization been successful in dealing with returning expatriates? Has reverse culture shock been an issue for many of these people?
- What was your first big "aha!" moment about the new culture you encountered?
- What characteristics would you look for in people who are more likely to be successful in an expatriate assignment?
- How do you believe HR departments should handle these assignments?
- How has living abroad affected you? What did you learn? Have you changed?

19

Leader of the Pack
The Thrill-Seeker in the Workplace

When Lawrence Devon, the VP Sales of a large retail group, was asked to see the CEO urgently, he knew the request was not good news. Obviously, he had done it again. Why did he always manage to get himself into such muddles?

People who knew him viewed Lawrence as the quintessential sensation-seeker—someone who liked taking risks. At times, his colleagues wondered how he was able to manage his tumultuous lifestyle. To all appearances, he seemed to be able to tolerate more chaos in his life than most people. But he also had the ability of keeping his cool when things got tough. Unfortunately, the way he behaved made him very difficult to manage. True to form, when life in the office became too predictable, he let everyone know that he was bored and looked for ways to stir things up. Many people in the office thought that his bosses only tolerated him because of his stellar sales record. Lawrence had always been one of the best (if not the best) at acquiring new customers. He also was well known for thinking "outside the box." He was viewed as one of the most creative people in the company.

Unsurprisingly, his private life was chaotic. Lawrence was acknowledged to be a fun-loving, chain-smoking, heavy-drinking gambler.

M.F.R. Kets de Vries, *Riding the Leadership Rollercoaster*,
DOI 10.1007/978-3-319-45162-6_19

His wild parties and womanizing were notorious. The accounts of his vacations were always a source of entertainment. Lawrence was into extreme activities, including hang-gliding, skydiving, and bungee-jumping. His passion for racing cars had almost killed him. If that wasn't enough excitement for several lifetimes, he had also had two short and stormy marriages. There were rumors that he had always been into high-risk sexual behavior and had multiple sexual partners.

Recently, however, his personal life had intruded shockingly in the workplace when one of his colleagues made a public scene about Lawrence's involvement with his wife. The incident got the attention of the CEO. Now she was wondering how to deal with Lawrence. Should she let him go?

Do you like exploring unknown places? Do you enjoy doing scary things, risky and adventurous activities and sports that provide unusual sensations? Do you go in for wild parties, drinking, drugs, and sex? Do you like to associate with people who are unpredictable but exciting? Are you allergic to routine activities?

If most of your answers to these questions are in the affirmative, you may have something in common with Lawrence. You may stand out from the crowd. You may be into thrill-seeking—someone who searches for new and intense experiences and feelings. You may be attracted to taking risks. The psychologist Frank Farley labeled people like Lawrence the Type T, or thrill-seeking, personality. Some of us have a low boredom threshold and are easily stimulated. Type Ts, have a much higher boredom threshold and need bigger thrills before they are aroused. T-personalities are addicted to risk-taking, stimulation, excitement, and arousal. Only by taking extreme risks, or engaging in disinhibited behavior, do they obtain the exhilaration they are looking for.

Long before the T-personality acquired some renown, the psychiatrist Michael Balint distinguished between two kinds of people, which he named the ocnophiles (non-adventurous types) and the philobates (thrill-seekers). They can be seen as extreme positions on a spectrum of neurotic conflict. Psychologically, philobatic behavior can be viewed as a form of self-medication, enabling these people to distract themselves from unpleasant feelings of depression or anxiety.

Unlike Balint, some neuroscientists have suggested that the question of whether someone is a thrill-seeker or not could be genetically based rather than a developmental issue. There is some evidence that sensation-seeking may have a genetic component and may be linked to various hormones and neurotransmitters. However, the basic architecture for what we will become is in place when we are born; the eventual outcome very much depends on environmental exposure.

According to these neuroscientists the brain structure of high-sensation seekers might be different from that of risk-averse people. This difference may explain why thrill-seekers are driven to overindulge in addictive substances or activities that stimulate their neuro-receptors. For example, we could hypothesize that thrill-seekers like Lawrence have fewer dopamine receptors in their brains to record sensations of pleasure and satisfaction. To feel good, they may need higher levels of endorphin activity. As endorphins are responsible for feelings of well-being, as well as pain relief, it is not surprising that people like Lawrence are into thrill-seeking. Their level of testosterone may also be influential, as testosterone seems to correlate with uninhibited behavior.

People like Lawrence are adrenaline junkies. They like to live on the edge. They need to flirt with death in order to feel alive. And some of these thrill-seekers use their personality for the good while others do the opposite, even engaging in sociopathic behavior. They may turn to crime, violence, or terrorism—just for the thrill of it.

So how can we deal with these people? How can we try to help them fit into society at large? How can we channel the positive aspects of their character and lessen the negative aspects? How can we get the best out of them?

Sensation-seekers like Lawrence will always have problems with more regulated society. Their behavior is bound to cause a certain amount of conflict. At the same time, given their taste for adventure, many Type Ts have the ability to attain the highest levels of creativity and innovation in science, business, government, and education. However, people who decide to hire them should be aware of what they are in for. T-personalities can cause havoc with respect to organizational processes.

On their part, thrill-seekers need to be very careful in selecting work that will fit them. They are highly susceptible to boredom, dislike repetition, routine and dealing with people who are not stimulating, so creative solutions need to be found to channel their considerable energy constructively. They will flourish in positions involving novel, stimulating, and unconventional activities—unstructured tasks that require a high degree of flexibility.

People who manage T-personalities should not take their disorganized behavior personally. They need to accept that some people are good at being organized, but aren't very creative. Others are very creative, but completely fail at being organized. The challenge is to help them structure their lives better, while allowing space for the more spontaneous aspects of their personality.

It can make a difference to enlist the help of co-workers with complementary skills, creating an effective executive role constellation in which the sum is greater than the parts. It is also a good idea to limit the responsibility T-personalities have for managing others; management is unlikely to be one of their strengths.

After the revelation of Lawrence's latest transgression, his considerable talents were not enough to keep him in his present company. In this case, he was no longer salvageable. We can only hope that he took his dismissal as a learning opportunity, the beginning of a journey to combine his considerable talents with some behavioral modification. His ability to adapt easily to changing situations, roll with the punches, and dare to find creative solutions could be used to great advantage in any organization.

Questions

- Do you continually crave new experiences? Are you always looking for new excitement? Are you prepared to break the rules?
- Do you like risk-taking? Do you like to do scary things?
- Which do you prefer, friends who are predictable or those who always surprise you?
- Are you sexually adventurous?
- Do you get bored quickly without high levels of stimulation?

- What do you prefer: novel, stimulating, and unconventional activities and unstructured tasks requiring flexibility? Or structured, well-defined tasks involving order and routine?
- Have you figured out what kind of organizational environment is most suitable to you, given your thrill-seeking style?

20

Shine, Shine, Shine

On Being a Star Performer

Over the years I have observed that organizational high-flyers are often a study in paradox. They display many contradictory behavior patterns. But it's precisely their paradoxical behavior that makes them so successful. Spotting nascent stars can be a real challenge, however, not least because we can't always be sure what we're looking for. Some may impress us as "golden larvae" but never turn into butterflies. Others are butterflies who can suddenly emerge out of nowhere.

What makes the larvae that turn into butterflies so special? What are the qualities that turn them into top performers? Is it luck or their connections that gets them where they are? Or are they just the right people, in the right place, at the right time?

Many leaders assume that stardom is somehow innate. My observations may help tease out some common myths about star performers and help us recognize their puzzling qualities. Successful executives come in many different shapes and sizes. Although highly successful people have many qualities in common, context matters. Just as there is no baby without a mother, there is no star without a constellation. Stardom very much depends on the highly complex interface between stars, the kinds of peo-

M.F.R. Kets de Vries, *Riding the Leadership Rollercoaster*,
DOI 10.1007/978-3-319-45162-6_20

ple they work with and the context in which they work—the political situation in a country, the national and organizational culture, the nature of the industry, the lifecycle of the organization, the state of the economy, and so on.

Having listened to the narratives of thousands of highly successful executives, I can confidently assert that stardom is not a matter of luck; it's a question of choice, and beyond that, of cause and effect. Although chance can be a factor, it is not a sufficient explanation. The old saying, "The harder I work, the luckier I get," contains more than a grain of truth. The stories I am told by top performers suggest that their "luck" is a combination of preparation, persistence, and opportunity. Top executives usually put a considerable amount of hard work and preparation into positioning themselves to grab any opportunity that comes their way, and so increase their chances for stardom. They also know how to positively reframe difficult situations.

Neither is stardom merely a question of having the right connections. Connections can be very helpful, but many very well-connected people turn out to be highly unsuccessful. Most stars achieve stardom because they have an intuitive understanding of how to make it happen.

In my experience what differentiates stars is their operational mode. They are walking contradictions; they have a knack of reconciling opposites. The psychologist Carl Jung used to refer to "*mysterium coniunctionis*," the alignment, joining, or resolution of conflict between poles or dualities that define human beings—the ability to hold the tension of opposites.

True stars have the creative ability to manage a short-term and long-term orientation, action and reflection, extroversion and introversion, optimism and realism, control and freedom, holistic and atomistic thinking, hard and soft skills. In addition, they are great at visioning, possess a solid dose of emotional intelligence, take calculated risks, are accountable for their actions, have great tenacity, high energy, and make a heroic (although often unsuccessful) effort to attain some form of life balance. Furthermore, stars seek out the unfamiliar—they are curious, imaginative, and insightful. They have a wide span of interests, and are open to new experiences. They like to play with new ideas; they find familiarity and routine boring; they have a great tolerance for ambiguity. And they are prepared to take a detour from the tried-and-tested, just because it is different.

What's more, their behavior can be contagious; others are inspired to follow their example. Given their specific mindset, stars are more inclined to give people who work for them the opportunity to experiment. They are willing to give others multiple chances and the benefit of the doubt. Stars can make decisions quickly, but can also be extremely cautious. They are rebellious and conservative, playful and responsible, reflective and proactive. They like to be sociable but also need to be alone; they are highly imaginative but maintain a solid sense of reality. And they are both divergent and convergent thinkers. Stars have the ability to switch from one mode to the other.

The good news for anyone aspiring to stardom, or those out stargazing, is that top performers can be made. Without discounting nature altogether, nurture plays a very important role. Stars are not born. Many of their psychological factors and behavioral characteristics can be learned. When we are young, our personality is very malleable, and early experiences carry much weight. And if the right foundation is in place at that stage in life, later developmental activities go a long way toward creating stars. The developmental experiences of top performers—their genetic inheritance and their early role models, combined with significant events during their childhood—weigh heavily in their personal and professional progress. They create the foundation for stardom.

I have been studying top performers for the past 40 years. The year-long CEO seminar that I have been running for more than two decades offers me holistic, in-depth psychological portraits of top performers. It provides me with a wealth of data, and gives me the opportunity to observe stars in an intimate setting. In acquiring this information I have also been helped by data obtained about them (and others) derived from a battery of "720°" feedback instruments, incorporating feedback from colleagues at work, friends, and family members—including children. These instruments have given me rich information about the personality and behavioral patterns of star performers in multiple contexts. These have helped me understand the paradoxical nature of their behavior.

But having identified potential stars, how can you make the most of them? How can you develop them? My observation suggests that to develop stars, the most effective strategy is to engage in self-assessment, action learning, and role modeling (shadowing). Of course, coaching them while they take these initiatives will be helpful. And the best approach is to use all these types of intervention simultaneously.

The journey to stardom begins inwardly. Self-awareness is one of the most important factors in building self-esteem and confidence. Self-awareness helps us understand what drives us, what turns us off, what make us happy, and what we are passionate about. It helps us clarify what we need to do to improve as a person. Greater self-awareness helps us acquire a more realistic sense of our capabilities. We will know when we are not using our full potential. We know what aspects of ourselves we need to work on. With greater self-awareness, we will be able to expand our imagination, creativity, intuition, will, and purpose. And an ideal method to jumpstart greater self-awareness is the use of multi-party feedback, a method of systematically collecting and rating perceptions of our performance from different vantage points. I have found that multi-party feedback—especially in a team setting—is unsurpassed as a means of setting developmental processes in motion.

Action learning is a process of bringing together a group of people with different levels of skills and experience to analyze an actual work problem and develop an action plan, using their jobs as the basis for learning. This is a reversal of the traditional model of learning, which takes people off the job for courses and external instruction. Action learning is learning by doing, or learning on the job. Through this kind of learning process, executives learn more about their own and others' way of solving problems, with a group dimension added. Action learning is a great way for high performers to practice working with important real-world problems as a basis for learning. As for the future stars, they are taken out of their comfort zone and given the chance to work and learn collaboratively with other high potentials.

Most of us learn by example, and learn most from the role models we observe in our earliest work experiences. Our bosses at this period in our life are those we will remember best. While it is obviously more attractive to learn from good bosses than bad, many future stars have also learned from the bad ones. These less than happy experiences may teach them how *not* to approach leadership—what things they should avoid doing to others. By observing experienced executives tackling their day-to-day duties, these stars in the making can look and learn, asking questions as they go along and bringing their professional studies to life.

Over the years, I have listened to the narratives of many stars, and I have learned that the only true failure is not having attempted a challenging developmental journey. The only way of discovering the limits of the possible is to venture a little way past them into the unknown. Excellence is not an event—it needs to become a mindset. It is doing common things in uncommon ways. It is the desire always to do things better. To be successful, we must break out of our comfort zone and learn to become comfortable with the unfamiliar and the unknown.

Questions

- How much energy do you put into knowing yourself better? Do you believe you manage yourself well? Are you prepared to subject yourself to a multi-party feedback exercise?
- Do you believe that your personal values are aligned with the values of your organization?
- Are you passionate in everything you do? Do you invest a lot of energy in everything you do?
- Are you always prepared to take on tough, challenging assignments?
- Do you have a panoramic view of your organization? Do you also zoom in to get a better idea what is happening "in the trenches"?
- Do you know how to positively reframe difficult situations?
- Do you have the courage to make really tough decisions?
- Do you believe you have integrity? Are you trusted by the people you work with?
- Do you see yourself as a team player? Are you a good networker? Are you helpful to others when needed?
- Do you allow people to make mistakes? Do you admit responsibility if you make a mistake?

21

Making the Best of It

On Happiness

Carl was unhappy and he had been for a very long time. He was unhappy with his work, with his life, with the world, and, most of all, with himself. Carl was a fully paid-up member of the self-pity club. His view of the world had always been dark. He was a pessimist and moaner who believed he was fated to have bad things happen to him. Life was unfair and he was its victim. Others were much more fortunate than he was and he envied them. He hardly helped himself by never expressing any gratitude to people who were kind to him. His wife was thoroughly fed up and at her wits' end. None of her efforts to accommodate Carl seemed to be good enough.

Things were no better at work, where Carl was VP Sales. His negativity was legendary within the organization. He never complimented people on work well done. Wherever he turned up, his presence lowered morale, affecting productivity—he seemed to have a knack of getting the worst out of people. His colleagues continually reminded him about the benefits of a positive approach, but to no effect.

The fact was that Carl didn't like his job, which he had drifted into. But when he was asked if he would be interested in finding a position that would give him more satisfaction and meaning, his response, predictably,

M.F.R. Kets de Vries, *Riding the Leadership Rollercoaster*,
DOI 10.1007/978-3-319-45162-6_21

was "mission impossible." He had always avoided taking risks. He also worried a great deal about money, and that any change in his position might have negative financial consequences. Very few things interested him—drinking alone in the local bar the one sorry exception. Most who knew him regarded Carl as a tragic figure who had never stretched himself to his full capacity or reached his full potential.

Carl's story raises a number of questions. Why are some people contented with their situation in life while so many others appear to be unhappy? What differentiates these people? Do people make themselves unhappy?

Significantly, when people are asked what they want out of life, in most instances happiness is at the top of their list. It is one of the most important—if not the pre-eminent—goals to which we aspire in life.

When we think about happiness, most of us envisage the good life, freedom from suffering, flourishing in whatever we are doing, prosperity, feeling well in ourselves, being aware of joy and pleasure. In general it boils down to something very much in line with the old Chinese maxim that happiness is "something to do, someone to love, and something to hope for."

Happiness is not an enduring state: it is made up of short moments in time, here one minute, gone the next. The more we pursue it, the more it slips away. It is not a destination to arrive at, but is made up of the experiences we have on the journey. In many instances, happiness and sadness run parallel to each other. It seems that in order to experience real happiness, we also need to have been touched by real sorrow, so that we can recognize happiness for what it is in the intervals between periods of unhappiness. Aristotle made a distinction between *hedonia*, which meant to him immediate pleasure—the in-the-moment experience—versus *eudaimonia*, which he described as a life well lived, the reflective experience of being content with one's life.

Evolutionary psychologists use the image of the hedonic treadmill to explain why increases or reductions in happiness (after significant events) eventually return to a set point. Any gains in happiness are temporary, because we quickly adapt to the change. Regardless of what happens to us, our level of happiness will return to our emotional and psychological baseline.

These intra-psychic dynamics suggest that without the existence of the hedonic treadmill, our species would have become extinct. Our expertise in rationalizing is our survival aid. The human brain has the unique ability to project into the future (thanks to the functioning of our frontal lobes) and the outlook, from wherever we stand, is not exactly positive. Therefore, for the purpose of our psychological health and continued survival, it's essential for Homo sapiens to have a happiness baseline that's set to positive.

Given the evolutionary element of this hedonic treadmill, we can assume that genetics has a major influence on happiness. Some researchers suggest that the inheritability of feeling well has a set point of 50%. There are two further variables to consider, as well as genetics. The first is our personal circumstances, the events that take place in our life. Childhood trauma or post-traumatic stress (following extreme experiences, like war or injury) will be counterproductive to the subjective experience of happiness. The second, which is given prominence by positive psychologists, is our intentional activities, estimated to have a set point of 40%.

These studies suggest that we have the capacity to make choices that will affect out happiness. Much of our capacity for happiness lies within our power to change. This means that if he felt so inclined even Carl has it in himself to be a great deal happier.

But what makes people happy or unhappy is not merely a matter of personality. It is also related to the kind of society we live in.

According to the World Health Organization, 1 in 20 people suffers from depression, a global number of 350 million, and in the USA 1 in 10 Americans aged 12 and over is taking anti-depressant medication.

These unhappy statistics have even encouraged the publication of a World Happiness Report that takes into consideration factors like real GDP per capita, life expectancy, social support, perceived freedom to make life choices, freedom from corruption, and generosity. The latest "winner" in the rankings is Denmark, while Burundi sits at the bottom of this list.

Not surprisingly, the countries with the highest levels of unhappiness are conflict-ridden, affected by economic, political, or social upheaval, or a combination of all three. In comparison, direct democracy, and the possibility of influencing our society and government, enhances our quality of life. We can deduce from the World Happiness Report and similar surveys that basic freedoms are essential for happiness.

Interestingly enough, a nation's human capital (social structures) and natural capital (nature) may be more influential in determining happiness in a society than financial capital (income). It's incorrect to assume that people with more money are happier than others. The correlation between income and happiness is modest. Our happiness starts to level off, in spite of a growing GDP. It seems that after we have sufficient resources to fulfill our basic needs (food, shelter, clothing), having more money becomes less important.

In fact, it's possible that adding money to money may lead to our experiencing less happiness. A preoccupation with material goods can become personally harmful. People can become bound to an acquisition treadmill (propelled by feelings of unhappiness and insecurity), piling acquisitions on acquisitions. Acquisitiveness is associated with a wide range of problems of psychological and physical health.

Material wealth is a relative concept. Even people who have considerable wealth and a high income feel compelled to compare themselves with others who are better off. As social creatures, our sense of self-worth and happiness derives in part from comparisons with others—groups or individuals we feel we should be equal to, or strive to emulate. Perceived prosperity is relative, as we only feel prosperous if we do better than the people with whom we compare ourselves.

Where there are considerable differences, there are likely to be greater levels of unhappiness. Serious income imbalances between layers of society will have a negative effect on societal happiness. Various studies have pointed out that happiness is lowest in countries that have the largest gaps between rich and poor, and higher in countries with smaller differences.

So, to what extent can we pursue happiness? Can we increase our likelihood of being happy? If so, what steps can we take? What hope is there for Carl and others like him?

Our freedom to engage in intentional activity suggests that there are several things we can do to improve our state of happiness. Happiness studies show that, as far as possible, we should avoid dwelling on the negative aspects of life. Unhappy people could make a greater effort to manage negative thoughts and emotions (anger, spite, envy, etc.) and try to foster positive thoughts and attitudes (empathy, serenity, and gratitude). Carl's negative mindset suggests that he's not going to find it easy to make these changes and is going to have to do some homework. So far, he's been busy counting his troubles rather than his blessings, so he could make a start by addressing how to lead a more purposeful life. He could look for activities that fit better with his values and interests. He could also consider ways to create happy moments. Instead of being the passive victim of his negativity, and resorting to getting drunk as entertainment, he could try to be more active and actually *do* things. While action may not always bring happiness, there can be no happiness without action.

Carl should also work at building and rebuilding relationships, so that he can spend quality time with friends and family. Good relationships are a sine qua non for happiness. Once he becomes more positive in his way of relating to others, people will be more attracted to him, and he will discover that happiness is a people magnet. Part of this rebuilding process might involve distancing himself from people who are stress inducers or otherwise unpleasant. Sometimes it is no bad thing to end a dysfunctional friendship. It can stop us returning to a place where we shouldn't have been in the first place.

Counting our blessings—making a conscious effort to practice gratitude and be thankful for the good things in our life—can work wonders for our mental health. Happiness is often a by-product of an effort to make someone else happy. If Carl could make himself reverse the lens through which he views his life, he might surprise himself with what he sees.

It can be liberating to discover that, while we cannot always be happy, we can create happiness—for ourselves and for others. And it is well worth the effort: happy people are healthier people who function at a higher level and use their personal strengths, skills, and abilities to contribute to their own and others' well-being. Another plus is that they live longer. Furthermore, happy people are more likely to contribute to the moral fiber of society in diverse and beneficial ways—economic, social, moral, spiritual, and psychological.

Our degree of personal happiness is heavily influenced by the choices we make, our inner attitudes, the way we approach relationships, our personal values, and our sense of purpose. We are largely responsibility for creating our own happiness. It's important to realize that the happiest people don't necessarily have the best of everything; they are the people who *make* the best of everything.

Questions

- Have you built a network of people whom you like? Do you see them regularly?
- Do you exercise regularly, and make sure that you have enough sleep?
- Do you make an effort to do a number of kind things every day?
- Do you write "thank you" notes to people who have a positive influence on your life?
- Do you regularly make time to get out into nature?
- Do you take time out to engage in conscious self-reflection?
- Do you regularly disengage from digital devices?
- Do you keep a diary that includes notes to yourself of what has gone well during your day?

Part III

Just Rolling …

22

Black, White, and Gray
Coping with the Bivalent Leadership Style

Most who knew her agreed that Joan wasn't the easiest person to deal with. She quickly got on people's nerves. Of course, her behavior wasn't all bad. As one of the senior executives in the company, she had a number of excellent qualities. She was creative, she had a great capacity for work, and she was extremely knowledgeable about the industry. So why, with all that talent, did she need to engage in so much drama? Why was she so rigid in her outlook? Why the angry outbursts, the constant criticism of everything and everyone, the half-truths, rumor spreading, and manipulation? Why did she always force everybody to choose sides? Didn't she realize that—in most situations—there is such a thing as the middle ground? But "compromise" didn't feature in Joan's vocabulary.

Joan had what can be described as a bivalent leadership style. Hers was a world of stark contrasts, where everything was similarly "split." She would only deal with the people she perceived as "good," and lost no time in vilifying those she perceived as "bad." The consequence of this behavior was intense strife wherever she went.

Joan's toxicity permeated the organization and might have continued unchecked had it not been for the shock impact of a 360° feedback report, administered as part of an assessment exercise for the company's executive

M.F.R. Kets de Vries, *Riding the Leadership Rollercoaster*,
DOI 10.1007/978-3-319-45162-6_22

body. The report revealed the extent to which Joan's colleagues and direct reports were fed up with her dysfunctional behavior. According to their feedback, the disturbances she was creating in the organization was driving everyone crazy. Her behavior was also highly contagious, and causing problems throughout the organization.

Based on the 360° feedback, Joan's boss laid it on the line. As far as he was concerned, Joan needed to change her behavior or there was no question of her getting the promotion she was expecting. At the same time, recognizing Joan's qualities and contributions to the success of the company, he arranged for her to work with an executive coach to support her change efforts. That's where I came in, as I had previously worked for the CEO of the company.

Initially, I hesitated about taking on the assignment. I knew from past experience that working with executives with a bivalent leadership style like Joan's could be a challenge. They are notoriously resistant to coaching interventions, as they quickly interpret any attempt at behavioral change as an attack. People like Joan can drive their coaches crazy just as much as their colleagues and direct reports.

If coaching was going to be successful, it was vital to build a stable, positive relationship with Joan. However, her three failed marriages didn't inspire confidence in her relationship-building skills. It was clear that Joan's way of splitting the world into good and bad had also led to a great deal of misery in her personal life. It was my awareness of this that persuaded me to take on her case.

The tactic of splitting people into enemies and friends is as old as human nature. Human beings have always been tempted to define the cosmos as a struggle between the good world of light, and the evil world of darkness. This sort of splitting extends into the everyday world. Everywhere we go, we thrive on black-and-white narratives such as good versus bad, negative versus positive, hero versus villain, friend versus enemy, believers versus unbelievers, love versus hate, life versus death, fantasy versus reality, and so on. Religions are more than ready to split the world into believers and non-believers, Christians against Jews, Muslims against Christians; similarly politicians' simplistic soundbites create the stark contrasting camps of Republican versus Democrat, Tory versus Labour.

Like most behavioral patterns, splitting originates in childhood and the way parents deal with their children. The tendency to split is related to insecure or disrupted attachment behavior patterns—bearing in mind that attachment behavior is the template of all human relationships. Learning how to be effective in interpersonal relationships is a journey that starts early in life and depends very much on the quality of the original child–caregiver relationship—how the caregiver interacts with the child. When the child reaches the developmental milestone of tolerating ambiguity, the foundation for emotional and social intelligence is established. However, if the child is exposed to too much strife and discord early in life, fuzzy, unstable boundaries can be created, making it more likely that the developing child will engage in splitting and categorize people and situations as either all good or all bad.

Splitting, or all-or-nothing thinking, is the failure to integrate the positive and negative qualities of the self and others. It means the inability to reconcile contradictory attitudes and to accept that we can have simultaneous positive and negative feelings about someone or something. And although splitting is a fairly common defense mechanism, for some people, particularly those with developmental issues, it becomes *the* defense mechanism. This position gives them clarity, of a sort. They are able to make clear distinctions, taking a confusing mass of experience or information and dividing it into categories that become meaningful. But the cognitive distortion brought on by viewing a multifaceted complex world through a binary lens means that we are bound to miss out on essential details.

My immediate challenge in dealing with Joan was how to help her recognize that living in a dichotomous world was self-defeating. She needed to move forward and have a more nuanced view of life. First, Joan had to acknowledge that she had very little understanding of her own inner thoughts, beliefs, desires, and intentions. This in turn made it extremely difficult for her to interpret other people's desires and motives. She needed to become more skilled at reading her own and other people's minds, to see others from the inside and herself from the outside.

Trying to help Joan was like walking on thin ice. I had to be very careful about how I gave feedback, knowing that she reacted very badly to criticism. For a long time Joan kept on splitting: I was good or bad, depending on whether I met her emotional needs or made her feel frustrated. She was completely unaware of her self-deception, selectively collecting evidence to support her oversimplified black-or-white perception of others. I kept on reminding myself that this was Joan's way of preventing herself being overwhelmed by anxiety. It was her way of protecting her feelings of self-worth. My task was to help her readjust this assessment and make the situations she encountered more reality-based.

Instead of focusing on her relationships at work, I got Joan to think about what was happening between the two of us. By concentrating on what was happening within the coaching relationship, and developing explanatory stories when something happened, she could contrast her perception of herself and her perception of me. The challenge was to increase her psychological sensitivity by exploring alternative interpretations and intentions from both her and my point of view. In fact, Joan needed to learn or relearn a number of things: how to empathize and make other people feel more comfortable; to communicate her thoughts and feelings clearly; and to control her feelings of fear, shame, and anger. It was particularly important for her to realize that her level of anxiety narrowed her focus so that she concentrated only on potential threats. Working together on these themes, however, we created a collaborative coaching relationship, in which both of us had a joint responsibility to understand the mental processes taking place in the here and now, and reflect on what had happened in similar situations before.

Gradually, Joan began to learn how to react to situations more appropriately. She started to pay attention to her mood swings and make an effort to stop and think about what was happening to her before reacting. Her impulse control improved. She came to realize that her bivalent leadership style meant that she was projecting her own fears and insecurities onto others. Slowly but surely, she became ready to accept that we all have flaws, that none of us is either black or white, and to let in the gray.

Outside our coaching sessions, two things were important additional supports for her change effort. First, Joan kept a diary in which she reflected on each day's events. This became an important aid in helping her see things from other people's perspectives. Recording her thoughts helped her become more effective at replacing negative self-defeating thoughts with more realistic ones. Second, Joan met someone and began a new relationship that had a stabilizing influence on her behavior. I was very encouraged by her ability to maintain this relationship and simultaneously make the effort to re-establish a number of old friendships. These secure relationships became safe testing grounds to help her understand the reasons for her previous disruptive behavior patterns and to adopt new, more productive ways of dealing with others.

Although the change was very gradual, Joan ultimately found a more effective way of living. After a year of coaching, I could confidently say that she was doing quite well and her progress was marked when she got the promotion her boss had ruled out 12 months earlier.

Questions

- How flexible do you think your thought processes are?
- Do you have a tendency to simplify the world by putting people into boxes, to classify them as "bozos" or insanely great?
- Is your leadership style characterized by black and white or all-or-nothing thinking?
- Do you find it hard to accept that the world exists of shades of gray? Are you willing to recognize that people can be both good and bad?
- Do you understand why you perceive the world in such stark colours? Do you have a sense of where this perception comes from?
- Are you the kind of person that believes that there is only one "right" way of doing things?
- When you have made up your mind, do you find it difficult to accept other points of view? Is it very hard for you to change your mind?

23

Fear of Failure or Fear of Success? Dealing with the Hannibals in the C-Suite

In 218 BCE Hannibal undertook a *tour de force*, crossing the Alps with 45,000 men and 70 elephants, in one of the most monumental feats in military history. His strategic brilliance, daring, and aptitude as a leader made him one of the greatest military commanders of all time. His decisive victory at the Battle of Cannae against a significantly larger Roman army is the stuff of legend. Where Hannibal fumbled was his failure to seize the big prize: Rome. Although he had several opportunities to do so, Hannibal never chose to attack and conquer the city.

Hannibal's indecisiveness at this crucial point has remained one of the baffling mysteries of military history. Instead of making a determined effort to take the city, Hannibal just waited. If he had advanced, he could have sacked and dismantled Rome in the way the Romans later laid waste to his home city, Carthage. Instead, for a period of 15 years, he and his army roamed Italy and conquered much of the countryside, remaining undefeated despite being outnumbered in combat. Eventually, a Roman counter-invasion of North Africa forced Hannibal to return to Carthage, where Scipio Africanus decisively defeated him at the Battle of Zama.

From a psychological point of view, the interesting question is why didn't Hannibal take advantage of his success and invade Rome when he

M.F.R. Kets de Vries, *Riding the Leadership Rollercoaster*,
DOI 10.1007/978-3-319-45162-6_23

could? This lack of resolve was especially strange as, from an early age, his father had instilled in him a deep hatred of Rome. According to a number of sources, Hannibal had promised his father, "I swear so soon as age will permit … I will use fire and steel to arrest the destiny of Rome."

Historians have come up with many rational, strategic excuses for why Hannibal didn't engage in direct war with Rome. The most popular excuse was that there was a lack of commitment from Carthage to provide men, money, and materiel—principally siege equipment. Without a permanent supply base, Hannibal wouldn't have had the resources to feed his animals and men for very long. However, one of the historians of that period, Livy, noted that if Hannibal had just shown up, the panic in Rome would have been so great that the city would have surrendered and no sustained siege would have been necessary.

Was there a more deeply hidden component to Hannibal's behavior? Was he fundamentally afraid of success?

I occasionally come across twenty-first-century Hannibals in organizations. Tim was typical. After graduating from an Ivy League college, Tim joined one of the premier strategic consulting firms as an associate. He was pretty effective in that role, and decided to do an MBA, graduating top of his class. After graduation, he joined a pharmaceutical firm, where he quickly rose in the ranks and joined the executive team in record time. However, when he was selected to succeed the CEO things started to fall apart. Tim began to procrastinate about making important decisions. He put off important projects or tasks in order to deal with issues of lesser importance. His hesitation to make important decisions lost the company key opportunities. His reputation took a further hit when he started to show up drunk at meetings with important stakeholders. Although initially the members of the board gave Tim the benefit of every doubt, they got to the point where they felt that they had no choice but to fire him.

Why had Tim, who had been a star performer in his previous jobs, become dysfunctional once he was top dog? Why was this ambitious and talented man unable to thrive as CEO?

Depressed after being fired from his job, Tim asked to see me. Listening to his story, it became clear that the root of his apparent fear of success stretched way back to his childhood. The dread of doing too well in life was clearly rooted deep in his unconscious. Digging deeper into Tim's story, I discovered that he was consumed by the idea that being successful was fraught with danger. It was too much tied up with his relationship with his father. Throughout his whole career, a self-imposed sentence of being unworthy of success had lurked around the edges of his life.

I gathered that Tim's father hadn't been very successful in life; numerous business endeavors had failed and these setbacks had made him a very bitter person. Worse, his father had always been very critical of Tim, making it quite clear that he didn't think Tim had what it took to be successful. Over time, Tim had internalized his father's assertions. This debasing sense of self remained latent in him until he reached the CEO position. While he had been able to keep his anxiety under control in less visible managerial positions, being in the top job brought things to a head. His subconscious would tell him that it was unacceptable to do better than his father. Therefore, after having done so, he was no longer able to control his secret self-image as an unsuccessful, undeserving individual and, unconsciously, he set out to sabotage his own career.

The fear of failure is intuitively understandable. In societies obsessed by success, failure is regarded as a catastrophe, and to some extent we all fear it. Ironically, however, we're also driven by the fear of success, a much more mysterious force. Many years ago, Sigmund Freud tried to demystify some of the dynamics behind this fear in an essay called "Those Wrecked by Success." He noted that some people become sick when they fulfill a deeply rooted and long-cherished desire.

The fear of success can comprise fear of our own greatness, evasion of our destiny, or a way of avoiding exercising our full talents. We hold ourselves back in subtle, often unconscious ways when we're suddenly in a position to achieve what we have always wanted. We may (unconsciously) fear the fame, fortune, and responsibilities that come with success. Success often raises others' expectations of us and increases the pressure to perform at a high level at all times under the critical gaze of others.

The heart of the problem could be that success singles us out from the crowd. I've encountered many high-flying executives who function extremely well as long as they aren't in the number-one position. But the moment they're placed in the spotlight, they are in uncharted territory and can no longer hide behind someone else. Moving up the ladder, they're legitimately worried about the increasing responsibility and visibility success will bring. Being in a more senior position, expectations are higher, scrutiny and criticism increase, and dread of being exposed is intensified. They may be faced with the challenge of having to constantly outperform themselves. Success can also bring a host of very tangible challenges, such as loneliness, new enemies, longer working hours, and isolation from the family.

The fear of success may also be rooted in subconscious family dynamics. For example, some people symbolically equate success with a victory over their parents or early role models. This is particularly true for people who have never satisfactorily resolved rivalrous feelings toward parents or siblings. For them, success is simultaneously desired and feared: desired because they want to supersede their role models and feared because, secretly, they do not believe they deserve it. For example, being a successful CEO might have been Tim's ultimate Oedipal victory, involving doing far better than his father.

Would it have been psychologically possible for Tim to learn to accept that doing better than his father was all right? Would it have been possible for him to accept that becoming CEO was not the end of the road and that there would be many new challenges ahead?

Going back to Hannibal, was he psychologically unable to accept doing better than his father? Is that why he failed to destroy Rome? We could speculate further and wonder if, having taken Rome, Hannibal would have felt there were no challenges left?

We will never know what motivated Hannibal's lack of action, but the next time we see someone snatching defeat out of the jaws of victory, we might remember Hannibal and Tim and consider what else might be going on in that person's inner theater. Changing irrational fears about success is possible but the first step is to recognize such self-defeating behavior. Facing his fear head on might have helped Tim. He could have spent time trying to understand the source of it. With honesty and self-insight, he might have realized that his self-sabotaging activities were undermining the achievement of his goals and dreams. And if Hannibal had had a therapist or coach to remind him of his own achievements and abilities, enabling him to free himself of irrational fears or echoes of the past, would he have moved forward and entered Rome? Unfortunately, we will never know.

Questions

- Do you procrastinate over activities that would make you successful?
- In situations when you have been successful in reaching your objectives, how did you feel? Did you feel anxious?
- At times, do you wonder whether you deserve to be successful? Are there occasions when you feel like an impostor? Do you believe that your work is never good enough?
- Do you think you're able to handle success? Are you worried that success might turn you into someone else?
- Do you worry that you might become vulnerable? Does the idea of success seem like entering dangerous, uncharted territory?
- If successful, would you feel exposed? Do you wonder whether being in an exposed position would make others envious?
- Are you concerned that success will imply that you are expected to be successful again? Are you worried whether you would be able to handle this pressure?
- Do you wonder whether success will change your private life, involving breaking ties with the people you know?

24

Why Do We Do What We Do?

Self-Knowledge

In 600 BCE, Greek sage Thales of Miletus observed that the most difficult thing in the world was "to know thyself." His observation is as true today as it was then, and is even timelier now, as Sigmund Freud's theories about unconscious mental processes are being rediscovered. Freud used the metaphor of the iceberg to describe the human mind. The part seen above the water is the conscious mind but the bulk of the iceberg lies unseen beneath the waterline and represents the unconscious.

Contemporary neuroscience has affirmed many of Freud's assumptions, suggesting that we are ignorant of ourselves due to the operation of unconscious mechanisms that determine largely how we feel and how we act. Much of what needs to be done for us to function is done unconsciously.

In management, the fact that we are ignorant of why we do what we do is expressed in the dichotomy between what executives say they do, and what they actually do. When I listen to what executives tell me, and see how they act, there is a remarkable gap between their intentions and their behavior. Why this gap exists, and why so many executives are completely unaware of it, is quite troublesome.

M.F.R. Kets de Vries, *Riding the Leadership Rollercoaster*,
DOI 10.1007/978-3-319-45162-6_24

A major contributing factor to this gap is that all of us are narcissistic to a degree. If we are truly honest with ourselves, we all believe we are special. This is a remnant of our evolutionary history. For reasons of survival, it must have been an advantage to be perceived as special. But the reality of what we are all about tends to be quite different. There may not be much that is special about us. We make enormous efforts, however, to prevent such cognitive dissonance from raising its ugly head; we do everything in our power to protect ourselves from possible narcissistic injuries. Buttressing our sense of self-worth is a lifelong endeavor.

People in leadership positions need the recognition provided by others to maintain their sense of self-worth. Taking an evolutionary, developmental perspective, these narcissistic strivings may once upon a time have been an essential factor in the survival of our species. Clearly, narcissistic behavior could have a significant reproductive payoff.

But behind this glorious façade, we are also quite an anxious lot. Admitting vulnerability, deficiency, or culpability doesn't come easily to most of us. This basic insecurity explains the existence of the elaborate defense system we use to ward off any sign of weakness and maintain our sense of specialness. These defenses are important, as they help us to avoid feelings of depression and to maintain the self-esteem, confidence, and optimism needed to keep us motivated. They explain why the main themes in our inner theater (most of them played out unconsciously) are attempts to avoid vulnerability and seek approval.

The principal reason why we are often unaware of the contradiction between what we say we do and what we really do is that we are trying to protect ourselves from the fear of embarrassment or threat, of feeling vulnerable or incompetent. Most of the time, our conflicting behavior should be seen as a consequence of opposing forces that are acted out in our unconscious. The push and pull of these forces are responsible for the gap between our good intentions and how we really behave.

To illustrate this puzzling issue, we can ask why so many executives have a need to control others. What holds them back from letting go? This kind of behavior generates a considerable amount of stress. It leads to micro-management and difficulties with delegation. Even when executives with this leadership style are made aware of the problem, they still remain resistant to change. Year in, year out, executives get the feedback that they are micro-managers and need to find better ways of dealing with their people. And year in, year out, these people promise to change but nothing happens. They are stuck. In the meantime, the executives talk a good game about what they are doing. They insist that they *do* delegate; they say that they allow for small failures; they say that they let their people get on with it. But in reality, they don't. So what is really going on?

The answer is that these people don't know how to edit the scripts in their inner theater. They continue to say all the right things and to do all the wrong things. They seem compelled to revert to the unconscious behavior that protects their sense of self-worth.

Most models of human behavior are built on the faulty assumption that we make decisions by consciously weighing all the relevant pros and cons. But most of the time, we do nothing of the sort. Instead, we act on the basis of a number of basic, unconscious rules that can sometimes produce completely baffling results.

As an executive coach and psychoanalyst, I have learned from experience that a 360° feedback exercise is a good start to help us recognize the gap between our imagined and our real behavior. A 360° feedback intervention can help us see what others have been seeing for a long time. It can help us to identify the areas we need to work on and throw up a number of indications of what makes our behavior so inconsistent.

Accepting that there is a gap between our intentions and actions helps us to reflect on what prevents us doing what we say we want to do. We can do a cost-benefit analysis of continuing or discontinuing some behaviors and devise an early warning system to subvert the power of our unconscious, which will try to make us revert to our preferred fallback position. Whatever efforts we make to do things differently, however, they will involve a lot of practice. It takes time to internalize new ways of doing things. It is very easy to relapse into old habits.

An executive coach or psychotherapist can support us in these change efforts and help us with coping strategies to avoid relapses. But in closing the gap between actual and desired behavior, we need to remember that if we want to see a change for the better, we have to take things into our own hands. It's simply not true that it's the thought that counts. People are judged by their actions, not their intentions.

Questions

- How aware are you of your cognitive distortions—your biases? At times, do you exaggerate your self-importance? In your personal case, are historical truth and narrative truth often far apart?
- To what extent do you realize that your behavior is not always rational?
- Do you assess people by what they say or by what they do? Which of these has the greater impact on you?
- Do you sometimes skirt the truth when a question you are asked has a societally acceptable "right answer"?
- Have there been situations when you were surprised about the difference between others' perceptions of you and your own perceptions?
- Do you believe that you walk the talk and practice what you preach?

25

Keeping it Real
The Need for Authenticity

Visitors to the Boston Museum of Fine Arts can admire Paul Gauguin's most famous painting, "Where do we come from? Who are we? Where are we going?" The huge canvas depicts a variety of figures, all Tahitian, each engaged in a particular and significant act, raising symbolic questions about the human condition. Gauguin intended the painting to be read counter-intuitively from right to left, and it depicts three stages in our life journey—birth and childhood, adulthood, and old age and impending death.

Gauguin made many transitions during his own life. Born in Paris, his family moved to Peru while he was a child but later returned, and Gauguin settled into a comfortable bourgeois existence as a stockbroker. He had discovered his talent for painting but for several years remained a Sunday painter, despite his contact with established artists like Pissarro, Cézanne, and van Gogh. His increasing disillusionment with material wealth and the business world led him to look for an unspoiled society and in his early forties he left his wife and children and moved to Tahiti where he began his second career as a painter.

Gauguin was in search of authenticity. His adult life was a continuous movement away from convention and artificiality toward the primitivism

M.F.R. Kets de Vries, *Riding the Leadership Rollercoaster*,
DOI 10.1007/978-3-319-45162-6_25

that he believed would make him happy. This is a journey in reverse, compared with that of many of the executives I encounter as an educator and executive coach. Most of these young men and women are in pursuit of *more*—more things, more money, more recognition, in order to do more of what they want so they will be happier. Many executives seem to forget that life is not all about power, position, and money. The challenge is to discover that how they spend their time is more important than how they spend their money. While it is good to have an aim, many executives fail to realize that the journey is all, and the end nothing. Most of us discover that arriving at one goal is just the starting point of a journey to another. It is the day-to-day experiences that count. The purpose of life is to live it, not to plan to live it later. We need to seize the day.

There is a Zen parable about a man who came across a tiger. He fled for his life, with the tiger chasing him toward a cliff. As he fell over the edge, he caught hold of a wild vine and broke his fall. The tiger continued to sniff and roar at him from above. Terrified, the man looked down: on the shore far below, another tiger had appeared, licking its chops. A slighter noise drew his attention. On a ledge a little way above him two mice were busily gnawing at the vine he was swinging from. Within arm's reach was a strawberry plant with one luscious berry growing on it. Grasping the vine with one hand, the man picked the strawberry with the other. How sweet it tasted!

Life exists only in the here and now. The past is gone, the future does not exist, and if we do not consciously live in the present moment, we are not really in touch with life. We cannot go back and start again, but anyone can start today and make a new ending.

However, authenticity is not necessarily easy. Gauguin's quest for authenticity cost him his career, marriage, family, friendships, and any chance of social acceptance. Achieving authenticity implies a willingness to accept who and what we are, and not attempt to pass for something or someone else. It implies taking off our masks. It means not only trusting our strengths but also facing our weaknesses and being patient with our imperfections. It means having the courage to say how things are, to say no, to face the truth, and to do the right thing because it is right. It also means letting go of the things in our lives that are false and don't really matter. It has to do with being genuine, not acting a part, not wearing a mask.

Many executives take the easier route of self-deception and illusion but find that it's not sustainable in the long run. If we don't tell the truth to ourselves, how can we be really authentic toward others? The problem with being inauthentic is that whatever we say or do will come back to haunt us.

When authenticity is grounded within, it affects all our interactions; it is like a diamond that marks all other surfaces. Authentic people inspire confidence in others and raise their spirits. Showing genuine concern for others provides "containment"—a safe place that helps others cope with conflict and anxiety.

Authenticity means being credible and trustworthy and abhorring hypocrisy in ourselves and others. When we can trust in ourselves we can have trust in others and establish meaningful relationships. That trust also gives us the courage of our convictions in difficult situations, helping us to remain faithful to our values and beliefs, rather than bowing to every pressure that comes along.

Authenticity implies doing things we really believe in, activities that reverberate with our needs, values, and dreams—in short, activities that have meaning and make us feel useful. Too many executives go through life like sleepwalkers without any real sense of usefulness because they pursue meaningless things.

With authenticity comes wisdom. Both are closely related human dynamics that reinforce and build on each other, and both focus on our existential journey. Wisdom is the reward for those who have encountered and surmounted difficult life experiences: it implies an understanding of the human condition.

So how can we be authentic? How can we acquire wisdom? In more religious periods of our history, people spent much of their time in worship. Prayer was an opportunity to reflect on life and take stock. Nowadays, although the need for quiet moments with ourselves is just as valid as it was in the past, such structured activities are far less routine. Yet we all need time for self-renewal and self-reflection. We need time to be alone, to examine what we are doing, and to think about what's right and good for us. We need time to examine our strengths and weaknesses. We need time to let our imagination fly. We need time to dream.

However, it is not always possible to arrive at self-reflection alone. Paradoxically, we may need professional intervention. We may need to consult someone who will help us make sense of our dreams and fantasies, get us unstuck when we're caught in a vicious circle, help us to see crucial links between past and present, and guide us into a better future. Dialogue of this sort is often uncomfortable. Because it requires opening up to another person to an extent that we don't often experience, it demands tremendous trust. But finding a companion for our journey of self-discovery can pay great dividends in terms of personal growth, seeing new alternatives, and pre-empting errors that would haunt us later in life.

Many people lack the courage to embark on such a personal journey. They run away from self-discovery—and can't stop running. Socrates once said that the unexamined life isn't worth living. We could equally well say that an unlived life isn't worth examining. If we are serious about the pursuit of wisdom, and leading an authentic life, we have to make the journey worthwhile, cherishing each moment.

There is another Zen story, about a woman who had been told about an enchanted valley, far away, full of the most beautiful flowers. She decided to go and see this magical place for herself. Although she set off eagerly, she quickly became disheartened at the length of the journey. Days turned into weeks, weeks into months, and months into years. Finally, she arrived exhausted at the edge of a forest where she found an old man leaning against a tree. She said to him, "Old man, I have been traveling now for longer than I care to remember looking for an enchanted valley, full of beautiful flowers. Can you tell me how far I still have to go?" The old man replied, "But the valley is right behind you. Didn't you notice? You passed it on the way."

As this parable tells us, it's important to focus on the route, the scenery, and our fellow travelers rather than on our destination. Too many executives spend their lives climbing ladders only to find that their ladders were placed against the wrong wall. We need to learn to enjoy the little things: they often turn out to be the big things in the end.

Questions

- Do you realize that if you try to be authentic, you may not be authentic?
- Do you believe that you are self-aware? Do you have a good sense of who you are—of your values, desires, inner motives, and what drives you?
- Do you act out of character—play roles—becoming different personas, depending on the situation? Are you aware that you are doing this? Do you feel uncomfortable when you are not true to yourself?
- Can you have a point of view, be courageous, have hard conversations, defending what you stand for? Or do you just not bother and go along with the crowd?
- Do you check in with your feelings and pay attention to your intuition when you are dealing with difficult situations? Does your intuition warn you when you feel out of sync between what you do and who you really are?

26

You Cannot Be Serious
On Gravitas

The two-horse succession race at the Rosen Company was reaching closure. The time had come when the candidates, Derek and John, would find out which of them would succeed the CEO. However, they knew nothing about the goings-on at the most recent board meeting. At one heated moment, during an intense discussion about their candidatures, one of the members of the selection committee had made it clear that she felt Derek was the more qualified of the two. Asked to elaborate, she said she thought John did not have the "gravitas" needed for the job. Given the challenges the company was facing, gravitas was top of her list of "must-have" qualities for the CEO. During a subsequent discussion, most of the other board members agreed, although none of them ever asked for a clarification of what she meant by "gravitas."

So what is gravitas? What does it look like in a leadership context? And how do we develop gravitas if it is such a critical factor in leadership?

Some wits have likened gravitas to pornography: you know it when you see it. For many, it refers to a mixture of poise, confidence, and authenticity. The word itself derives from the Latin *gravitas*, meaning weight, and *gravis*, heavy. It suggests that people who display gravitas are grounded, possess sound judgment, and are able to deal with weighty

M.F.R. Kets de Vries, *Riding the Leadership Rollercoaster*,
DOI 10.1007/978-3-319-45162-6_26

issues. For the ancient Romans, gravitas was the highest of the 14 virtues. Without gravitas it would be impossible to attain a reputable position in society.

Clearly, gravitas connotes seriousness of purpose, solemn and dignified behavior, and being perceived as important and compelling. It's something to aspire to, as these qualities are assumed to be associated with leadership effectiveness. In organizational life, gravitas is also seen as key to the ability to yield influence.

As our succession example shows, in the world of corporate advancement, gravitas is taken very seriously. Headhunters, talent managers, and HR professionals always ask themselves whether people have the gravitas required for a role. Do they have presence, speaking skills, and the ability to read an audience or situation? Do they have the emotional intelligence that enables them to influence others easily? Generally, the assumption is made that people with gravitas lead better, manage better, present better, and network better. And often, gravitas becomes the determining factor that makes or breaks careers. In this case, the lack of it became the main reason why John, despite his technical qualifications, was not selected for the top job. The directors were looking for someone they believed could hold his own in sometimes difficult or unprecedented situations, handle various stakeholders effectively, and make tough decisions. They were attracted to the person whose words would carry weight, who could speak with authority, was trusted, and was sought out for his opinions, insights, and advice.

At this point you may be wondering whether you have gravitas? Do you have presence? Are you considered a person of authority? Do people stop and listen when you speak? Do you know how to engage and influence others? If the honest answer to these questions is "no," is there something you can do about it? Is gravitas an inherent personality trait or can it be developed?

One way of tackling this is to make a distinction between the internal and external qualities of gravitas. I am not suggesting that these are rigid boundaries. The internal and external qualities interact with each other, making for a dynamic equilibrium.

Starting with internal qualities, to radiate true gravitas we need to have a modicum of self-awareness. Without self-awareness, and by extension, self-possession, we will never be able to master our emotions or discover the power within ourselves. As well as self-awareness, we need knowledge. After all, knowledge creates power. We need to be steeped in the topics that we talk about. By acquiring more knowledge and applying it correctly, we will add to our gravitas.

The external qualities of gravitas refer to how we are perceived by the outside world in acting, speaking, and looking. How we act will be determined by the degree to which our emotional intelligence enables us to stay cool, calm, and collected when faced with tough situations; we need to display courage and grace under fire. It also relates to our ability to read and analyze a situation and deal with it effectively. People with gravitas know how to act when things run out of control. They have the confidence and equanimity to deal with unpredictable situations; they know how to stand their ground when pushed into a corner.

How we speak is determined by our vision, our ability to communicate it effectively, and our ability to inspire others. Do you talk with passion and energy? Do you use an authoritative voice? Do you emanate integrity, trust, and respect? Do you keep your promises?

The final factor, how we look, is determined by our appearance. What is the first impression you give? How do others read your body language? Reputation is also part of how we look. It is critically important to have a stellar and ethically unblemished reputation.

Some of these characteristics can be developed easily, with coaching and skills intervention. Others may take decades of learning, requiring the wisdom that can only come through experience.

However, there are a number of quick wins that can be made at the superficial behavioral level. For example, you can look for opportunities to hone your presentation skills. You can learn how to speak on your feet. You can practice how to remain level-headed, regardless of the situation. You can learn how to acquire a unique voice. To help with this, you could ask for personal feedback from trusted colleagues, mentors, friends, and family members.

The inner journey, which touches upon personality, takes place over time through the accumulation of experience. Gravitas is often developed through life experiences and reactions to challenges and hardships along the way. The inner journey into the self to understand our strengths and weaknesses is certainly not a quick fix. It is laborious work, requiring constant self-reflection and incremental changes.

The best way to develop gravitas is to tackle the matter from both angles. People who pursue gravitas balance external appearance with internal solidity. They know the difference between appearance and substance and how to manage the dynamic relationship between the two.

Questions

- Do you believe that there is "central casting" for every situation? Do you act accordingly? Do you have a good understanding of how others interpret how you act, speak, and look?
- Do people switch off when you are speaking? Do they ignore what you are telling them? Do you know why?
- Have you ever received feedback about your body language? Do you pay attention to this particular aspect of how you present yourself?
- Do you know what you stand for, and do you have an idea how you will react to different situations and respond to them?
- Do you think that you have grace under fire, the ability to stick by your vision, and the emotional intelligence to answer knotty questions appropriately? Do you remain composed whatever the situation, whether you are glorified or vilified?
- Do you have the confidence, consistency, steadiness, and persistence needed in presentations? Do people take notice of you? Do you command respect, and hold the attention of others? Are your ideas and insights welcomed and embraced?

27

Just Write it Down

Writing as Therapy

In one of my leadership development workshops, Simon, a senior executive at an oil company, felt compelled to talk about an incident that he had never properly dealt with. He told the other participants about a harrowing experience he had had in Nigeria when he was held hostage during a visit to one of the oil rigs for which he was responsible. He recounted tearfully how during the hostage-taking, two of the other hostages—his close colleagues—were killed before his eyes. After long, drawn-out negotiations on the size of the ransom demanded by his kidnappers, he was finally let go. Although Simon was very lucky to escape with his life, the memory of what happened lingered on. From that moment, he had been plagued by nightmares of his terrible experience. But while recounting his story, he said that he had started to feel better since he had tackled one of the assignments in the workshop, which was to write a reflection paper about this difficult experience.

We all know that deliberately inhibiting thoughts and feelings about traumatic events requires great effort. The act of repression reinforces obsessive thinking and excessive rumination, resulting in cumulative physical stress and long-term physiological and mental problems. Moreover, the repression of painful memories has only a limited, short-term benefit.

M.F.R. Kets de Vries, *Riding the Leadership Rollercoaster*,
DOI 10.1007/978-3-319-45162-6_27

What's pushed away has a tendency to reappear in other ways. A more fruitful approach may be to confront and talk about painful experiences.

Josef Breuer and Sigmund Freud first explored the value of dealing upfront with traumatic experiences in their book *Studies on Hysteria*. In it, their famous patient Anna O. called this procedure the "chimney sweeping method" or the talking cure. Breuer would later refer to it as the "cathartic method." Taking a historical perspective, we can even look at the act of confessing or articulating and sense-making of trauma as part of the healing tradition found in many places throughout the world. This doesn't mean, however, that people, who talk about painful experiences will necessarily get better. Growth, healing, or a change of outlook all depends on individuals' interpretations of what has happened to them.

Like talking, writing about upsetting events seems to contribute to a new understanding of the events themselves. However, the act of writing engages a different part of the brain. Writing (like painting), mostly reaches the back part of the brain, the visual cortex, where images are produced. While spoken language is more related to the right hemisphere of our brain, writing appears to have a greater effect on the left hemisphere, stimulating parts of the brain that are not affected by talking.

Writing also gives a different voice to our confused interpretations by gradually pulling together the disparate fragments of thought, emotions, and ideas, weaving them into an intelligible whole. The confrontation and clarification of painful episodes through the process of writing involves translating the event into a meaningful narrative, enabling cognitive and emotional integration, contributing to a deeper understanding of what has happened. Writing about painful events seems to help us gain greater clarity of purpose, and greater freedom of choice. Contrary to the regressive process of repression, the writing process enables us to take charge of our own narrative and move forward.

The reflective writing assignment that helped Simon confront his experience is a pillar of the CEO leadership development workshop I have been conducting for many years. I have observed that although talking about difficult issues has a very cathartic effect, writing about them can have an even greater payoff. When we translate a difficult experience into language, we literally "come to terms" with it. Writing forces participants in the workshop to relate traumatic past experiences word by word, phrase by phrase. In this way, difficult experiences are broken up into small, manageable segments.

I am not alone in asserting that writing can have a stress-reducing and revelatory effect. A number of health psychologists have also focused on this subject, notably on how writing can be used in a variety of ways to heal emotional injuries, increase an understanding of ourselves and others, develop a greater capacity for self-reflection, reduce physiological symptoms, and alter behaviors and thinking patterns. The work of James Pennebaker, a research psychologist at the University of Texas, has been particularly illuminating. Pennebaker has conducted a number of controlled experiments to confirm the effectiveness of writing about emotional upheaval. What he calls expressive writing—writing about thoughts and feelings that arise from a traumatic or stressful life experience—has helped many people cope with the emotional fallout of such painful events. Expressive writing can also have long-term effects on diseases such as asthma, chronic fatigue syndrome, post-traumatic stress disorder, and arthritis. Pennebaker also discovered that when people write (or dictate) for approximately 20 minutes a day for three to four consecutive days (preferably at the end of the day), they require fewer medical visits than people who don't write (as many as half). Pennebaker's experiments also showed that not dealing with painful experiences created greater physical and emotional stress and placed people in a higher risk category.

Pennebaker makes the point, however, that people not only need to discover meaning in a traumatic memory, but also have to feel the related emotions to be able to reap positive benefits from the writing exercise. He also cautions that initial writing about trauma may trigger temporary distress and physical and emotional arousal, emphasizing that the timing of the writing experience matters. Some studies have shown that people who write about a traumatic event immediately after it has occurred may actually feel worse after expressive writing, possibly because they are not yet ready to face it. Pennebaker advises his clients to wait at least one or two months after a traumatic event before trying this writing technique.

In my experience, writing about difficult episodes in our lives helps us to move beyond brooding, create a new narrative, and generate new behaviors. Although writing is a solitary activity, it is also relationship building, in that we are writing for potential audiences. Writing leads indirectly to reaching out for the kind of social support that can aid the healing process. Thus, our social connections may improve, partly because we will have a greater ability to focus on someone (the reader) beside ourselves.

Nobody really knows exactly how the writing remedy affects the brain, but the answer probably lies somewhere in the strong connections between emotional stress and illness. But from what I infer from my work with executives, venting emotions alone is not enough to relieve stress and improve physical and psychological health. To tap into writing's healing power, we need to evoke, understand better, and learn from our emotions. For Simon, writing helped him to put into words feelings and anxieties that he had been unable to describe. Doing so cleared the way to help him resolve longstanding relationship issues at home and work. When people allow the pen or keyboard to take them where they need to go, surprising insights emerge. As the writer Anaïs Nin said, "We write to taste life twice, in the moment and in retrospect."

Questions

- Do you keep a diary? If not, what holds you back?
- If you keep a diary, are you in the habit of writing about stressful situations?
- When you write about stressful situations, does this activity help you talk about such incidents with others?
- Do you think that writing about stressful situations has helped you to break free of the mental stress of brooding or rumination? Has writing helped you to better understand and learn from your emotions, including finding meaning in a traumatic memory? Does writing help you understand why you are experiencing stress?
- If you are in a coaching or therapeutic relationship, is writing in between the sessions part of the therapeutic process?

28

Ecotherapy

On Getting Out and About

It had been quite some time since Jasper had felt his usual self. Ever since he had been promoted, and had moved to head office in the city, his mental state hadn't been the same. He was anxious and restless. He missed his old house in the country, daily walks with his dog in the woods, and being surrounded by nature. Now, the best he could do was a short walk in the nearest park, a subway stop away. But it wasn't the same. All it did was make his nostalgia for the woods more poignant. Jasper knew his current state of mind was affecting his motivation and the quality of his work. He found it a challenge to maintain focus, he made mistakes, and he was often in a foul mood. He was seriously questioning whether he would be able to hold on to his job.

According to the author of *The Nature Principle*, Richard Louv, people living in today's world often suffer from what he calls "nature-deficit disorder." Louv was referring to the negative behavioral consequences of our divorce from our natural habitat. Louv is not alone in expressing these concerns. There is a substantial body of research on the restorative benefits of connecting with nature. According to these studies, our mood improves dramatically when we spend time outside. Being in nature appears to reduce the stress hormones in our blood, our respiration rate,

M.F.R. Kets de Vries, *Riding the Leadership Rollercoaster*,
DOI 10.1007/978-3-319-45162-6_28

and our brain activity. It can affect our psychological mood states. It can help change a depressed, stressed, or anxious state of mind to one that is calmer and more balanced.

These findings make sense when seen from an evolutionary point of view. Being in nature has a strong primordial influence on our psychological and physical well-being. For most of us, being in nature—and a part of the wider collective human matrix—is a great escape from the pressures of modern life.

The counter-position, as Jasper was experiencing, is that when we feel alienated from the natural world we are likely to experience a range of personal, relational, and social problems. These include psychological disorders such as free-floating anxiety, depression, and other psychosomatic symptoms. Thus it should not come as a surprise that (according to numerous studies) urban dwellers with little access to green spaces are more likely to have psychological problems than people living near parks, or residents who make regular visits to natural settings. Even the simple addition of flowers and plants to a workplace can positively affect our ability to be creative, productive, and solve problems. Other studies have shown that contact with animals can reduce aggression and agitation among children and people diagnosed with Alzheimer's disease. Children who live close to green spaces seem to have better concentration, a greater ability to delay gratification, and are more effective in controlling impulsive behavior, compared to children who are surrounded by concrete. Regular contact with the natural world—whether it is through gardening, interaction with animals, nature walks, or nature brought indoors—contributes to our sense of self-esteem, social connections, health, and general feelings of happiness.

Most of us living in the urbanized, developed world have lost our connection to nature, however. Living in the Cyber Age has added to our sense of alienation. Ecopsychologists maintain this split between human beings and nature is at the heart of our current ecological crisis. Instead of respecting and reinforcing our fundamental ties with the Earth, we are destroying what remains of our planet. Our participation in the degradation of land, water, and air not only affects human health today, but will also affect the health of generations to come.

We need to return to an understanding that human and ecological well-being are closely intertwined. We need to start reversing our planet's continuing ecological deterioration. We need to act against the consequences of eco-stress—the sense of inner emptiness due to alienation from ourselves, others, and the natural world. We need to relearn how to care for our environment, and in doing so, learn to care for and nurture ourselves. This is where ecotherapy comes into the picture.

Ecotherapy, also known as nature therapy, can be viewed as a union between the ideas of ecopsychology and psychotherapy. It refers to the kind of mental health work that puts our connection with the Earth at the core of our psychological activities in order to restore our alignment with the natural world in which we live. Ecotherapy is a way of reinventing psychotherapy and psychiatry with the human–nature relationship at its core. With this approach, ecotherapy can help us to cope with the stresses and strains of daily life.

As a form of psychological intervention, ecotherapy is influenced partly by psychoanalytic object relations theory, social systems theory, and the psychology of religion. Object relations theory tries to explain the way we relate to others. It is suggested that the quality of our relationships with others and "objects" (including the way we internalize experiences with the natural world) are deeply influenced by our relationship with our earliest significant caregivers, usually our parents. Much depends on whether these internalized experiences were primarily positive and nurturing, or threatening and toxic. Social systems theory helps us to understand how we function not only in human systems but also within greater multi-species systems. Finally, the psychology of religion helps us understand how humans exist within the context of natural phenomena. Ecotherapy is interested in the examples provided by a wide range of ancient and contemporary indigenous cultures. Ecotherapy can be seen as a way of returning to our roots, rediscovering the way our ancestors have acted over thousands of years.

From my work with clients, I have learned that spending time in nature provides the space for inward reflection and recharging energy, increasing the potential for inner transformation. Immersed in nature, we become more conscious of our self in relation to our environment.

We return to a state of interconnectivity with the world around us. This (re)connection is powerful, as it may regenerate our spirits, improve our mood state, ease our levels of anxiety and stress, and help us to fight depression. Ecotherapeutic interventions can be used on their own, or can accompany other treatments, such as psychotherapy or medication.

But experience has also taught me that re-establishing a connection with nature can be an uphill struggle. Many people have become fully estranged from nature. To help them change, I often begin this form of therapy by asking my clients to keep a nature journal, recording how much time they spend in the outdoors and describing their physiological and psychological states when there. I advise my clients to hike, take up gardening, or engage in other outdoor activities. I may hold some counseling sessions outdoors so that they experience the benefit of nature while getting some clinical help—a walking and talking cure. I also encourage them to travel to wild places. Being in vast and immense landscapes (mountains, seas, plains, forests) reminds us of our "smallness" and prompts a sense of awe and wonder for the world in which we live. Thus, it becomes an excellent antidote to excessively narcissistic behavior. Experiencing heightened senses and greater connectedness between self and the world around can lead to intense spiritual and transcendental awakening.

So, the next time your mood is low, put on your hiking boots. I didn't hesitate to suggest to Jasper, given his psychological make-up, that he would do well to reassess his ambitions and consider whether he should return to a place where, as the French say, he felt "good in his skin."

Questions

- Do you spend time outdoors, swimming, camping, walking, and just enjoying being in nature? Does being outdoors increase your feelings of well-being, reduce your level of stress, improve your concentration, and make you more relaxed?
- If you live in a city, do you make an effort to walk in a park, have plants in your office, or keep animals? Do you try to create some green space around you?

- Do you work (or are active) outdoors (i.e., gardening, farming, fishing, watching wildlife, camping, or hunting)?
- Do you believe nature reduces your self-centeredness?
- Have you ever had a spiritual experience as a result of exposure to nature? Does being out in nature help you feel connected to other living things and understand your interdependence with them?

29

Sweet FA
The Art of Doing Nothing

Hélène runs a large organization in the educational field. I was curious about her working habits and asked her how many emails she received every day. "Five hundred," she said, then continued in a rather upbeat manner, "Frankly, I don't read any of them. If I did, I wouldn't really be doing my job. My job is to think about the future of education in my country. These days, given the work I do, it isn't a question of obtaining information. The more important question is how to push information away so that I don't suffer from information overload. I need to have time to think."

What I liked about Hélène's comment was her realization that she needed a considerable amount of time out to reflect, be creative, and to tackle larger issues such as the vision and direction of her company. This required her to make a conscious effort to resist the impulse and distractions of manic activity and to dedicate time for creative inactivity. Paradoxically, and against popular mindset, slacking off—making a conscious effort not to be busy—may be the best thing we can do for our mental health.

However, in a society driven by the cult of overwork, the balance between activity and inactivity has become seriously out of sync.

M.F.R. Kets de Vries, *Riding the Leadership Rollercoaster*,
DOI 10.1007/978-3-319-45162-6_29

In contemporary organizations work addicts are highly encouraged, supported, and even rewarded. The practice of doing nothing, by contrast, carries a stigma of irresponsibility, wasting time, and the social pressure of not living up to performance expectations, especially when others are clocking up time. We have been conditioned to the point that we feel guilty and restless if we don't have something to do. Just look around you—on the train, in the street, and even in meetings—people are glued to their mobile devices, constantly receiving or transmitting information. The danger of being constantly available, however, is that we may lose our connections, not just with one another but with ourselves. If we don't allow ourselves periods of uninterrupted, freely associated thought and reflection, personal growth, insight, and creativity are less likely to emerge. And in the long term, our general well-being will also suffer.

Keeping busy can be a very effective defense mechanism to ward off disturbing thoughts and feelings. But by resorting to "manic" behaviour we suppress the truth of our feelings and concerns, consciously or unconsciously. Yet unconscious thought processes can generate novel ideas and solutions more effectively than a conscious focus on problem solving.

One of the benefits of taking time out is that it creates the opportunity for play. The functions and benefits of play (unstructured activity undertaken for pleasure and exploration rather than a specific goal) have been studied for decades. Evolutionary psychology has long emphasized the adaptive functions of play. Unfortunately, as adults, many of us have unlearned our early natural state of play. Replacing creative freedom with logic and structures, we have left the sandbox and forgotten the importance of spontaneity. Like doing nothing, play in the adult world is perceived as unproductive and a guilty indulgence.

I argue that play is not a luxury, but a necessity. It taps into rich emotions and states that are beneficial for personal development and well-being. It facilitates discoveries and connections, and evokes feelings of surprise, pleasure, and understanding. Play also helps relieve stress. It triggers a mix of endorphins that lift our spirits and help us cope with pain, fear, and anxiety. Play can also help us manage grief. In fact, the benefits of play for both children and adults are too many to mention, which makes it not only a frivolous but also a very serious business.

Doing nothing and boredom are closely intertwined and both get a bad press. Complaints of frequent and persistent boredom are typically viewed as a sign of a flawed character. But is there really something wrong with us if we're bored? Because boredom, when we look at it more closely, has some unique values.

When we are bored we are subsumed by the feeling either that there is nothing do to or that what we are doing is an unrewarding non-activity. We are swamped by the urge to engage in something satisfying but are unable to do so. Boredom is a real factor in many aspects of domestic life and in jobs with limitations, such as highly repetitive service, functional, and assembly line work, and we need to be able to tolerate it. In fact, we are handicapped if we cannot deal with boredom constructively. People who respond to boredom reactively, with a continuous need for stimuli and thrills and a paucity of inner resources, can wreak havoc in the home and workplace.

In many instances, boredom can be a prelude to something. It can be a trigger for imagination and creativity and is closely associated with expectation. It might indicate a desire to seek out new and potentially more interesting and stimulating avenues. Reframed differently, boredom can be seen as a critical resource that pushes us to seek the unfamiliar. Being bored can help us to develop a rich inner life and become more creative.

However, most of us find it hard to tolerate boredom, especially as boredom is often associated with depression. Instead, we keep busy, and push our troublesome demons away—busyness makes us feel better and even virtuous. But what are we all busy about? Why are we running so hard? We're stressed, we're exhausted and half the time we're not even sure we're running in the right direction.

Doing nothing frees up mental space for reflection and problem solving. Novel connections or ideas often insinuate themselves into the conscious mind when our attention is directed elsewhere. Incubation, or the unconscious recombination of thought elements, requires the process of doing nothing and boredom. Subsequently, the solution often comes "out of the blue," when we least expect it. Many have discovered that such passive, unfocused moments are necessary for "Eureka" moments to occur.

Consideration of distraction and boredom brings us to the question of left and right brain activity. Neuroscientists have noted that "left-brained" people tend to be more logical, analytical, and objective, while "right-brained" people are more intuitive and reflective. The left side of the brain appears to be the seat of language and logical and sequential information processing. The right side tends to be more visual, and processes information intuitively, holistically, and randomly. And although the right hemisphere lacks the major elements of verbal language (processes controlled by the left brain), it uses the "language" of pictures, music, and emotions, which plays an important role in the creative process. The two sides of the brain need to work together, however, to perform tasks.

Keeping in mind this left–right brain division of labor, our more humdrum, daily activities are largely dominated by the left side of our brain. Busyness and left-brain activities are closely allied. Going through our usual routines in our waking hours (and under most circumstances), the more cognitive processes of the generally dominant left hemisphere will overrule right hemisphere processes. This doesn't mean that there is no simultaneous right-brain activity. However, it's particularly during periods of inactivity (when we are doing nothing or are being bored) that the right hemisphere seizes the opportunity to express itself. It really gets to work in situations of relaxation, meditation, hypnosis, fantasy inducement, or daydreaming (similar to what happens during the night while we dream). Thus, although right hemisphere processes are always hovering about, they do not have much opportunity to assert themselves when we keep ourselves busy. Doing nothing, or having nothing to do, are valuable opportunities for stimulating unconscious thought processes. Compared to conscious thought, unconscious thought excels at integrating and associating information and is capable of carrying out associative searches across a broad database of knowledge. In the region of the unconscious, we are less constrained by conventional associations and more likely to generate novel ideas.

It is important to have a place where we can take time out from our fast-track lives to play more fully; where we can engage in a dialectic, interactive process that enables us to experience both the freedom and the discipline to cultivate a sense of possibility and enhanced meaning. In practical terms, one way of doing this is to participate in the kind of transformational executive workshops and programs that take a psychodynamic (emotional and psychological) approach to further our development. These programs are given greater impetus by the fact that many people enroll because they sense that something is going on in their lives that they want time out to explore. They are mentally ready to set aside time for reflection and to find ways to do things differently.

As a form of organizational "play therapy," once a year, I run a workshop called The Challenge of Leadership: Creating Reflective Leaders. Twenty very senior executives from all over the world (most of them at CEO level) are invited to participate. The guiding themes may have to do with seemingly insoluble dilemmas, negative feelings about themselves, being bored, or feeling like an impostor. They may be suffering from various stress symptoms, or struggling with the existential dilemmas of life. Typically, however, these issues are not clearly articulated in the candidates' mind when they apply to the program.

The goal of the program is to create a transitional space for these executives to pause by stepping out of their everyday busyness into a space of reflection and experimentation. Throughout the program, a key element is nurturing a sense of play among the participants. This space provides a kind of holding environment in which the participants' dysfunctionalities can be contained and mirrored. Within the workshop, unconscious and unrecognized material, including long-repressed fears and longings, surface. This prompts classic forms of resistance, such as splitting, projection, denial, displacement, dissociation, and depression. As time goes on, these defenses become less effective. By the end of the program, most of the participants have broken down their barriers and are able to have the courageous conversations they have never had. Through the process, the participants also become reflective and self-analyzing.

In these interventions, I have seen the power of taking time out from the deadening and distracting effects of routines, rules, and the expectations of others. A transitional space is vital for the development of the self—whether this emerges as inhibition or the capacity to create—and for individual creativity and cultural experience. Through it, they can feel secure enough to return to a state of playfulness and spontaneity, to experiment with new challenges, explore new places, ideas, and activities, and to emerge with new perspectives and solutions. Even more importantly, the fruits of this process are brought back into their daily life, as participants begin to consciously integrate more reflective and meaningful behavior into their working life.

The time may have come for executives and organizations to return to the sandbox and recognize the power of doing nothing. To be more effective, we need to allow ourselves, and others, regular disconnection from busyness and schedule times in our day when we are completely free to reflect and think. Any activity that takes our mind off the problem at hand, that allows our thoughts to roam freely, or helps us focus on an entirely different activity, might do the trick. Only by "unthinking" can we really arrive at new, creative ideas. Seemingly inactive states of mind can be an incubation period for future bursts of creativity. A number of companies have turned to mindfulness and meditation practices to help their employees tap into their creative potential. 3M, Pixar, Google, Twitter, and Facebook have made disconnected time, or contemplative practices, key aspects of their way of working. The objective is to increase their employees' self-awareness, self-management, and creativity. The goal is to work smarter, not longer.

The most effective executives are those who can both act and reflect. If we don't know how to calibrate the balance between work and play, we may become casualties of physical and psychological burnout. Taking time to do nothing, however, will make us more productive and creative. As the saying goes, sometimes we need to fall off the mountain to realize what we have been climbing for.

Questions

- How good are you at saying "No" to make free time for yourself? Are you good at making "me-time"?
- Is it easy for you to play? Do you see yourself as playful? As an adult, do you often play with children?
- Are you able to "do nothing"?
- Do you get anxious when you do nothing? Do you only feel good when you are busy?

- Do you regularly switch off digital devices to have reflective time?
- Do you spend enough time sleeping?
- Do you pay attention to your dreams?

30

Dream Journeys

The Royal Road to the Unconscious

Lee, the CEO of an IT company, told me about a dream in which he was walking toward his summerhouse but then realized he was completely naked. The only thing he had to cover himself with was a very small towel. As he started to run home he noticed neighbors on their balconies laughing at him. Suddenly he tripped over, lost his towel, and spotted his wallet lying empty on the ground. He woke up feeling vulnerable and unprotected.

When I asked him what the dream meant to him, Lee made the association with how he always felt exposed at the annual shareholders' meeting—a meeting that was coming up soon. Although he did well speaking in public, it was not something he looked forward to. It had taken him quite some time to get used to this event. He also wondered if being nude in his dream meant that he was going to be caught off guard. Was he going to be accused of a cover-up—be exposed as a fraud? Was there going to be a proxy fight? He recalled that when he took over as CEO, he had promised a quick company turnaround but so far that turnaround was not forthcoming. The dream also made him realize that his greatest fear was to be asked to divest some of the company holdings (the empty

M.F.R. Kets de Vries, *Riding the Leadership Rollercoaster*,
DOI 10.1007/978-3-319-45162-6_30

wallet standing for resources being taken away)—something he viewed as a disaster for the future of the firm.

Sleeping and dreaming are essential parts of the human condition. We sleep for approximately 122 days out of every year. During the average night, we have one dream every 90 minutes. Most of us have three to five dreams per night but some of us may have up to seven. By the age of 60, we have dreamed approximately 90,000 hours with almost 200,000 dreams. And the dreams that occur during these night journeys—when taken seriously—can offer useful clues about our preoccupations and concerns. Reflecting on how these dreams relate to what's happening in our waking life can help us recognize and address some of our internal struggles.

The study of dreaming is called oneirology (from the Greek, *oneiron*, for dream), and it's a field of inquiry that spans neuroscience, psychology, and even literature. But while students of oneirology have proposed many theories about why we dream, no single consensus has emerged about the purpose of dreams, let alone about their interpretation. In the study of the mind, dreams remain one of the last frontiers, yet to be fully conquered.

Whether dreams actually have a physiological, biological, or psychological function is still open to many questions. However, most dream researchers believe that dreaming is essential for our mental, emotional, and physical well-being. Of course, there are some who suggest that dreams serve no real purpose. They view dreams as merely random and meaningless firings of neurons in the brain—neurological processes that don't happen when we're awake. There are many others, however, who have a very different point of view.

A promising angle in explaining why we dream is the evolutionary point of view. According to a number of evolutionary psychologists, in dreams we are actually rehearsing fight-and-flight responses. They suggest that the biological function of dreaming is to simulate threatening events, and to rehearse threat perception and threat avoidance. It's a way of preparing and coping with possible traumatic events. And taking this evolutionary point of view one step further, we could hypothesize that through the analysis of our dreams we may become more aware of things that we don't like to see or hear in daily life. Furthermore, if we have repetitive dreams or nightmares, we'd better pay attention.

It is not always easy to make sense of the language of dreams. Given the fact that dreams have their own language, ranging from the ultra-normal and ordinary to the overly surreal and bizarre, dream events can appear intensely real and full of meaning while we are dreaming, but leave us with a sense of discomfort when awake. I have found, however, that understanding these night-time meanderings can be a very powerful problem-solving tool, providing a short cut to better understanding the pressures and stresses affecting us in our daily lives.

As our lives are very intertwined with dreams, with their links to the unconscious (in the process weaving together action and reflection), dreams can also be viewed as a kind of psychotherapy—a form of story-telling, registering very subtle signs that may go unnoticed during our daily waking life. In dreams (in contrast to what's happening during our waking state), we deal with emotional content in a safe place, enabling us to make connections that we wouldn't be able to make if we left matters to the more critical or defensive parts of our brains. If we are to believe many psychotherapists, taking dreams seriously proves that we are missing something very important with every dream we don't remember.

Dreaming helps us think through emotional stuff in a less rational and defensive frame of mind. Dreaming enables us to gain insights about others and ourselves that otherwise remain repressed. Reflecting on our dreams, we may be able to see people and situations from waking life in a new light, identifying the hidden truth of various situations, which is usually disguised in a symbolic language mixed with visual and linguistic puns. Dreams may force us to ask ourselves difficult questions that we do not want to face. They provide clues to our internal struggles, behavior, and concerns and brings them to a more real level of awareness. Dreams may help us to see colleagues or family members through clearer eyes or act as a short cut to get to the essence of an issue or challenge. Also, dreams may help us to find creative solutions to everyday problems. In our dreams, we may find locked away the inspiration and answers to real-world problems. In addition, by reflecting on our dreams, we may be prepared to take the kinds of actions when awake to solve what may have first looked like unsolvable dilemmas. This explains why "sleeping on it" often can provide a solution to a problem.

A case in point is Elias Howe, the inventor of the sewing machine. He had an idea of a machine with a needle that would go through a piece of cloth but he couldn't figure out exactly how it would work. Exhausted by frustration he fell asleep and dreamt that savages in a strange place were chasing him. Native warriors caught him and threw him into a cooking pot. As he frantically tried to get out they poked him back in with their spears. He woke terrified but on later reflection remembered each spear had a hole through it like a huge sewing needle only in this case the holes were at the head not near the tail. Translating this idea into his machine and having the thread pass through the point of the needle was a major innovation, which led to the design of the first modern sewing machine.

Some people may have difficulty remembering dreams, but dream recall is a skill that can be learned. For example, it helps to remain motionless immediately after waking, letting thoughts drift and dream images surface. As a matter of fact, when waking from a dream, we have only a few precious moments before details begin to dissipate and memories fade. Again, we may be able to give an evolutionary psychological explanation for why this happens. Most probably, if the recall is too strong, we may get confused between our waking and sleeping state, a muddle that can have very negative consequences. Given the ephemeral nature of dreams, one way of retaining them is to keep a pen and paper or recorder beside the bed, and note them down before they evaporate. Just a few words that capture the essence of the dream will make the unconscious content more concrete.

Just as you may describe your dreams to others, they may tell you theirs. But keep in mind, when trying to make sense of other people's dreams, that they are *their* dreams—they are the director, producer, and scriptwriter of these nocturnal productions just as you are of yours—and it is up to them to decipher their own specific dream symbols. We all have our own dream "language." All dreamers have their own folds to open and knots to untie. A bear in a dream, for example, will mean something different to a hunter than it does to a child who claims it as her favorite stuffed animal. A car to a racing driver is something quite different than for someone who takes an occasional weekend drive.

The subjects, figures, animals, people, and unusual beings in dreams are there to help us and teach us about aspects of ourselves that have been ignored, unrealized, or forgotten. By examining each dream element and looking for parallels between associations, we can decipher a dream's meaning. Of course, what complicates this process is that before unconscious, fearful thoughts can be displayed, they may be censored—leading to a great deal of puzzlement. But even if initially the dream content doesn't make sense, by contemplating and meditating on the dream we may obtain greater insight about its message. Thus dreams can only be understood in the wider context of a person's unfolding life history.

The most important questions to ask while reflecting on a dream are "What immediate associations do you make with the dream?" "What does the dream make you think of?" "How does the way you feel in this dream echo in your waking life?" In other words, in what kind of waking situations have you felt similar emotions to what you experienced during the night? Asking these kinds of questions helps to decipher your own unique set of dream symbols—finding out what specific symbols in your dreams mean to you. But there isn't a set of stringent rules that needs to be followed when working with dreams, and there are no specific formulas or prescriptions. Every person and every dream is unique. In addition, all dreams may have multiple meanings and layers of significance.

Nearly two-and-a-half millennia ago, the Chinese philosopher Zhuangzi awoke from a dream of a butterfly and declared, "Now I do not know whether I was then a man dreaming I was a butterfly, or whether I am now a butterfly, dreaming I am a man." This much-quoted story underlines that much of our sense-making is bound up in apparent contradictions. Yet it can also be viewed as analogous to the enlightenment experience. Using dreams helps us to become more mentally awake—to reach a greater level of awareness—although we may have to go through the intermediary larval and pupal stages before we can become fully fledged butterflies. To quote Sigmund Freud, dreams really are the royal road to the unconscious.

Questions

- Is it easy for you to recall your dreams? Do you make efforts to remember your dreams? Have you found ways to increase your dream recall?
- Do you have repetitive dreams? Do you have nightmares? Can you recall your repetitive dreams and nightmares? Do you understand the significance of these dreams? Do you understand what these dreams are trying to tell you?
- When you recall a dream, do you spend time making some sense out of it? Do recurring dream symbols appear in your dreams? Have the associations you make with your dreams helped you to solve difficult problems?
- Do you share your dreams with others to help you make sense out of them, and vice versa?
- Do you try to control your dreams?

Index

M.F.R. Kets de Vries, *Riding the Leadership Rollercoaster*,
DOI 10.1007/978-3-319-45162-6

D

E

Q